THE ANATOMY OF THE CASE STUDY

Gary Thomas & Kevin Myers

THE ANATOMY OF THE CASE STUDY

SAGE

Los Angeles | London | New Delhi
Singapore | Washington DC

Los Angeles | London | New Delhi
Singapore | Washington DC

SAGE Publications Ltd
1 Oliver's Yard
55 City Road
London EC1Y 1SP

SAGE Publications Inc.
2455 Teller Road
Thousand Oaks, California 91320

SAGE Publications India Pvt Ltd
B 1/I 1 Mohan Cooperative Industrial Area
Mathura Road
New Delhi 110 044

SAGE Publications Asia-Pacific Pte Ltd
3 Church Street
#10-04 Samsung Hub
Singapore 049483

© Gary Thomas and Kevin Myers 2015
First published 2015

Editor: Jai Seaman
Production editor: Sushant Nailwal
Copyeditor: Kate Campbell
Proofreader: Jill Birch
Marketing manager: Sally Ransom
Cover design: Shaun Mercier
Typeset by: C&M Digitals (P) Ltd, Chennai, India
Printed in India at Replika Press Pvt Ltd

Library of Congress Control Number: 2014950843

British Library Cataloguing in Publication data

A catalogue record for this book is available from
the British Library

ISBN 978-1-4462-4863-8
ISBN 978-1-4462-4864-5 (pbk)

At SAGE we take sustainability seriously. Most of our products are printed in the UK using FSC papers and boards.
When we print overseas we ensure sustainable papers are used as measured by the Egmont grading system.
We undertake an annual audit to monitor our sustainability.

Contents

List of figures and tables

Figures

Tables

About the authors

Gary Thomas is a professor of education at the University of Birmingham. His teaching and research have focused on inclusion, special education and research methodology in education, with a particular focus on case study. He has co-edited the *International Journal of Research and Method in Education* and the *British Educational Research Journal* and is currently executive editor of *Educational Review*.

Kevin Myers is senior lecturer in Social History and Education at the University of Birmingham. He works on the history and sociology of education, and has specific interests in the application of psychological knowledge in school systems. He serves on editorial boards for the journals *History of Education, History of Education Review* and *Paedagogica Historica: International Journal for History of Education.*

Preface

Gerring (2004: 341) recently suggested of case study that 'Practitioners continue to ply their trade but have difficulty articulating what it is that they are doing, methodologically speaking. The case study survives in a curious methodological limbo.' This book grew out of a wish to help with the 'methodological limbo' by seeking the 'anatomy' of good case study – discovering its vital organs and how they work together. Part of the problem seemed to be that case study takes such varied shapes and sizes; as such it is difficult to get any sense of identity about what is, despite its mutable nature, undeniably a coherent design framework. If we could gain some sense of the structure – the essential ingredients – of this protean form of inquiry we could then, we hoped, offer intending inquirers a Gestalt from which to consider ways of going about constructing and critiquing it.

With Gerring's assertion in mind, this book aims to:

- provide integrity and coherence for readers on recent ideas about case study; and
- offer to tutors and advanced students theoretical insights that have implications for the design and practice of case study.

Adapted versions of certain chapters published here have appeared previously in print. Part of the reason for their publication in a book is to offer an integration and synthesis of the ideas offered therein and to present them with new connective and illustrative material. In particular, parts of Chapter 3 were published in the *Oxford Review of Education* (Thomas, 2011a) and Chapters 4 and 5, adapted for this book, appeared in *Qualitative Inquiry* (Thomas, 2010; 2011b). The case study abridged for commentary in Chapter 7 (Myers, 2011) was published first in *Paedagogica Historica*.

We are grateful to colleagues, friends and students at the University of Birmingham for their help, ideas and support, though any errors of fact or judgement are, of course, down to us.

Introduction

In writing a book about the anatomy of case study we intend to look at the way in which case study is constructed, at its necessary features and the way that these connect to make the case study succeed as a productive form of inquiry.

Our reason for thinking that such a project might be necessary came from the realization that what goes under the name 'case study' can sometimes amount to not much more than a weakly differentiated collection of thoughts and quotations from interviews with very little in the way of analytical binding (see Luker, 2008, for a discussion). As the design of the case study is presented often as open-ended and untethered to any methodological frame, researchers – particularly those researching their own practice – may feel unguided about structure. The consequence is that the putative case study can therein lack purpose, integrity or analytical grip on any theme.

The problems of case study

There are two central problems that the case study as a form of social science inquiry has to face.

The first concerns its supposed deficiency in generalizing 'power'. This problem can be addressed by looking at the notion of induction, and at what social science tries to do with this notion. It can be addressed also by questioning ideas about theory: as in most social science inquiry, case study is supposed to help develop theory, but little is said about the kind of theory that is supposedly developed. What exactly is it that we are developing?

The second is a more practical problem, and one that faces both novice and experienced researchers. It concerns the lack of structure surrounding this form of inquiry. What purposes can be served by the case study? Should case inquirers be seeking theory or trying to illustrate? Should they be looking retrospectively or at contemporary snapshots? Are multiple studies legitimate? And what is being sought when a case study is conducted? As Gerring (2004: 341) puts it: 'Practitioners continue to ply their trade but have difficulty articulating what it is that they are doing, methodologically speaking. The case study survives in a curious methodological limbo.' De Vaus (2001: 219) agrees, in discussing the way that the case study is explained: 'Most research methods texts either ignore case studies or confuse them with other types of social research.'

There is no comprehensive synthesis of literature about case study that helps with the 'methodological limbo' by offering any kind of classificatory typology for intending researchers. There have been only limited attempts to offer intending inquirers a Gestalt, mapping out the terrain and potential routes to travel.

This book brings together some ideas addressing both the epistemological and the practical issues concerning case study. We look at generalization and induction, asking whether what happens in social science research is not really induction, but rather abduction. We question assumptions about theory, separating theory from phronesis. And on the practical issue of classificatory schemata we overview some of the ways in which case study is discussed and defined in order to propose a framing structure and typology for case study (see Chapter 5 and Thomas, 2011b).

We thus intend in this book to provide integrity and coherence for readers on recent thinking about case study, and to offer to tutors and advanced students theoretical insights that have implications for the design and practice of case study.

What is in this book?

In the first chapter we examine and review definitions of case study, notably those from Simons (2009), Yin (2009), Flyvbjerg (2006), Mitchell (2006), George and Bennett (2005), Stake (2005), Hammersley and Gomm (2000), Bassey (1999), Ragin and Becker (1992), Merriam (1988) and Eckstein (1975). On the basis of these, we offer a new definition for the case study. The chapter will also unpick some of the inconsistencies in the literature on case study, noting in particular the ambiguities set off by Lijphart (1971) in his distinction of comparative study from the case study. Importantly, it will introduce a distinction between the *subject* and the *object* of the case study – one which will be amplified in Chapter 5.

Chapter 2 examines the place of case study in social science inquiry, tracing its modern historical roots to Frédéric Le Play and Jean Marc Gaspard Itard. It will also draw a distinction between Windelband's 'idiographic' and 'nomothetic' forms of inquiry, examining the history of the debate about holism versus particularity, and drawing on Flyvbjerg's tracing of the origins of the debate back to Athens. Various branches of holism will be discussed for their relevance for case study, from phenomenology and symbolic interactionism to Gestalt psychology and systems thinking.

In Chapter 3 we look in detail at the issues about generalization to which we have just alluded. Is generalization possible from case study? Arguments for the value of case study are undermined by assumptions about the need for generalization in the warrant of social scientific inquiry. But outside the discussion of generalization specifically in case study, commentary has pointed to the failure of social science generally to offer any special kind of generalization which can be shown to be more reliable and valuable than the everyday generalization of the layperson. The point we shall make is that if such critical commentary has validity, the failure is not unique to case study – it exists in all forms of social inquiry. We shall argue that case study's shortcomings in generalizability, far from minimizing case study's offer, in fact free it to offer something different and distinctive in social scientific inquiry. Thus, the potential of case study may be realized in developing something rather more nuanced than generalized knowledge – in what we here call exemplary knowledge. The latter, drawing its legitimacy from phronesis as distinct from theory is clearly different from generalizable knowledge.

Chapter 4 examines induction in case study. The validity of case study as a respectable form of social science inquiry rests in its ability, like other forms of inquiry, to use a form of induction in developing theory. Here, we argue that social science inquiry does not in fact use induction and does not develop theory in the conventional sense. Rather, it uses abduction and develops phronesis. The argument is that making distinctions clear between induction, abduction, theory and phronesis offers a pathway for the better conduct of case study and for a less apologetic stance in its use.

In Chapter 5 we attempt a typology of case study – an aim that was introduced in Chapter 1. We do this by disaggregating the various layers of classificatory principle for case studies which are discussed in the literature. We first distinguish two parts of the case study: i) the *subject* of the study, which is the case itself; ii) the *object*, which is the analytical frame or theory through which the subject is viewed and which the subject explicates. Beyond this distinction the case study is presented as classifiable by its purposes and the approaches adopted – principally with a distinction drawn between theory-centred and illustrative study. Beyond this, there are distinctions to be drawn among various operational structures that concern comparative versus non-comparative versions of the form and the ways that the study may employ time.

The next two chapters (6 and 7) open up the nature and anatomy of the case study by giving detailed examples. Chapter 6 aims to give shape to the typology drawn in Chapter 5 by drawing on examples which reveal that there are numerous valid permutations of the dimensions outlined in the typology and many trajectories therefore open to the case inquirer. Purposes have to be identified first (evaluative or exploratory), then approaches need to be delineated (theory-testing, theory-building or illustrative), then processes must be decided upon, with a principal choice being between whether the study is to be single or multiple, and choices also about whether the study is to be retrospective, snapshot or diachronic, and whether it is nested, parallel or sequential. It is thus possible to take many routes through the typology, with, for example, an exploratory, theory-building, multiple, nested study, or an evaluative, theory-testing, single, retrospective study. The typology thus offers many options for case study structure. In this chapter we give examples of case studies that take various routes through the typology, as a demonstration of the wide variety possible.

Chapter 7 offers a case study in far more detail, giving an edited version of a paper about a working class family in the 1930s which successfully resisted the pressure of the local education authority to send the youngest child of the family to a residential special school. It raises a range of issues, from eugenics to psychometrics to the use of authority and professional power. It brings these together to provide a rich analysis of the ways in which forces interplay to develop, enact or resist policy. The case study is offered as an exemplar, with an annotated guide to indicate its 'anatomy' and its categorization according to the typology offered in Chapter 5.

The final chapter attempts to integrate the main themes of the book and revisits the notion of 'anatomy' for case study. It picks up each of the themes – case study construction, theorization, generalization, induction – and it sets these together, noting that the integration of these themes is necessary for the success of this form of inquiry.

ONE
What is case study?

Definitions

Differing themes and priorities characterize attempts at definition of the case study. This is to some extent explicable by the diversity of disciplinary starting points from which practitioners and analysts of the case study arrive. While those from sociology, education and psychology have tended to see the case study in an interpretivist frame, those from business, politics and other areas may espouse the interpretivist holism of case study but address this through what George and Bennett (2005: 5) have called 'neopositivist' means via the identification of variables to be studied – see, for example, the discussions of Luker (2008) and Yin (2009). By contrast, those in medicine and the law have tended to see the case study principally as a vehicle for exemplifying or illustrating novel or archetypal phenomena.

Notwithstanding these differences, strong commonalities exist across disciplinary margins. Reviewing a number of definitions of case study, Simons (2009) concludes that what unites them is a commitment to studying the complexity that is involved in real situations, and to defining case study other than by the methods of data collection that it employs. On the basis of these commonalities she offers this definition:

> Case study is an in-depth exploration from multiple perspectives of the complexity and uniqueness of a particular project, policy, institution, program or system in a 'real life' context. (Simons, 2009: 21)

To Simons's definition, we should emphasize the point she makes in her preliminary discussion that case study should not be seen as a method in and of itself. Rather, as Stake (2005: 443) suggests, it is a design frame that may incorporate a number of methods and analytical frames – hermeneutic, organic or cultural. Choice of method, then, does not define case study: analytical eclecticism is the key.

Ragin (1992: 5) centres his definition on the case study's contrast with what we might call 'variable-led' research. Rather than looking at few variables in a large number of cases, the case inquirer looks at the complex interaction of many factors in few cases: the 'extensiveness' of the former is discarded for the 'intensiveness' the latter offers. There is a 'trade-off,' as Hammersley and Gomm (2000: 2) put it, between the strength of a rich, in-depth explanatory narrative emerging from a very restricted number of cases and the capacity for generalization that a larger sample of a wider population can offer. Ragin puts it thus:

> The ... case-oriented approach places cases, not variables, center stage. But what is a case? Comparative social science has a ready-made, conventionalized answer to this question: Boundaries around places and time periods define cases (e.g. Italy after World War II). (1992: 5)

Ragin's definitional discussion serves two purposes: it contrasts the emphasis on cases with an emphasis on variables in other kinds of research. In discussing the *boundary*, it also stresses the particularity noted by Simons and Stake – wherein the parameters of particularity are set by spatial, temporal, personal, organizational or other factors.

One important feature of cases only alluded to in the definitions discussed thus far is any emphasis on the significance of an *analytical frame* in the constitution of the study. For example, while the Korean War as a subject of study might satisfy conditions of singularity, boundedness and complexity, it would not be a case study – or at least not the kind of case study that would be of interest to social scientists – unless it could be said to be a case *of* something, and that '*of*' would constitute the study's *analytical frame*. The Korean War's status as a case *of* something has to be established. Is it a case of a war? If so, can it be said that it is a case of an especially remarkable or unusual *kind* of war? Perhaps, by contrast, it may be a case of a border dispute or of US resistance to the perceived threat of communist expansion. George and Bennett (2005: 69) put it this way: '... the investigator should clearly identify the universe – that is, the "class" or "subclass" of events – of which a single case or a group of cases to be studied are instances.' The subject of the study is thus an instance of some phenomenon, and the latter – the phenomenon – comprises the analytical frame.

Although writing earlier than George and Bennett, Wieviorka (1992: 159) showed that the case is not *simply* an instance of a class. He unpacked in more detail the distinctions between the case and the class by noting that when we talk about a case we are in fact talking about two elements: first, there is what he calls a 'practical, historical unity'. We might call this *the subject* – in the example above it would be the Korean War. Second, there is what he calls the 'theoretical, scientific basis' of the case (such as US resistance to putative communist expansion, in the same example).

This latter forms the analytical or theoretical frame, and we might call this *the object* of the study. The notion of a 'theoretical, scientific basis' thus delimits the 'class': the class has to offer more than a set of similar instances. So, the class cannot comprise merely similar phenomena (for example, wars) but those phenomena as instances of an analytical focus (for example, resistance to perceived communist expansion). Wieviorka continues:

> For a 'case' to exist, we must be able to identify a characteristic unit ... This unit must be observed, but it has no meaning in itself. It is significant only if an observer ... can refer it to an analytical category or theory. It does not suffice to observe a social phenomenon, historical event, or set of behaviors in order to declare them to be 'cases'. If you want to talk about a 'case', you also need the means of interpreting it or placing it in a context. (Wieviorka, 1992: 160)

We shall return to issues of definition and to the crucial difference between the subject and the object of the study in Chapter 5. Suffice it to say for now that we take the subject–object distinction to be critical for an understanding of the purpose and conduct of the case study. Alongside holism and methodological eclecticism, case inquirers need carefully to consider the nature of what is being studied, analytically speaking – they need, in other words, to consider the *object* of their studies. It is for this reason that we offer our own definition incorporating these elements (subject and object), as follows (and we go more fully into the details of this in Chapter 5):

> Case studies are analyses of persons, events, decisions, periods, projects, policies, institutions or other systems which are studied holistically by one or more methods. The case that is the subject of the inquiry will be an instance of a class of phenomena that provides an analytical frame – an object – within which the study is conducted and which the case illuminates and explicates.

Singleness

Singleness is the watchword with case study: case study is about the examination and analysis of a single phenomenon. The phenomenon may be a person, a group, an institution, a country, an event or a period in time. The researcher may be looking at the process of a medical diagnosis with one patient, or at a gang of teenagers, or at one student's learning in class, or a family, or at the development of a business, or the USA's political stance at the time of the Cuba missile crisis. Any of these phenomena could form the subject of a case study. What is of interest is the uniqueness of the phenomenon and the phenomenon in its completeness.

Case study concerns an understanding of *how* and *why* something may have happened, or why it might be the case. The assumption in a case study is that with a great deal of intricate study, looking at the subject from many and varied angles we can get closer to the 'why' and the 'how'. We have to look at our subject from many and varied angles, to develop what Foucault (1981) called 'a polyhedron of intelligibility'. By this he meant that inquiries in the humanities and social sciences are too often one-dimensional, as if we are looking at our subject just from one direction. In looking from several directions a more rounded, richer, more balanced picture of our subject is developed. A three-dimensional view is observed and appreciated.

The key is in doing what Flyvbjerg (2001: 132) calls 'getting close to reality'. By this he means thinking with your own experience and your own intelligence – and it is this that case study is particularly good at encouraging, for it eschews methodological formulae and endorses and stimulates a critical, creative approach to problem solving. Flyvbjerg proceeds to put the emphasis in this 'getting close to reality' on 'little questions' and 'thick description'. We sometimes ignore these little questions in the 'Big Science' version of what research should look like. Flyvbjerg (ibid: 133) quotes Nietzsche as saying, '… all the problems of politics, of social organization, and of education have been falsified through and through … because one learned to despise "little" things, which means the basic concerns of life itself.' As Flyvbjerg points out, small questions often lead to big answers.

The truth of Flyvbjerg's point is exemplified in an exemplary case study – *A Glasgow Gang Observed* (Patrick, 1973). It was written by a young sociologist who had infiltrated a gang in the Maryhill district of Glasgow. By joining the gang and becoming a participant in its activities, Patrick paints a detailed picture of the ways in which it operated. Although it is a case study – there is only one gang, not 50 from which to generalize – it gives, through sparkling analysis, an understanding of gangs. Even though there is no pretence that this is a representative picture, or that all gangs are like this, we nevertheless garner a rich understanding of the dynamics, tensions and motivation of gangs.

Flyvbjerg (ibid: 135–6) puts it thus:

> … practical rationality and judgment evolve and operate primarily by virtue of deep-going case experiences. Practical rationality, therefore, is best understood though cases – experienced or narrated – just as judgment is best cultivated and communicated via the exposition of cases … which is why … John Dewey [says]: 'the way to re-enchant the world … is to stick to the concrete.'

Much can be achieved in the recourse to the concrete. The inquirer can escape from a tendency too often found in academic writing to obfuscate with abstractions rather than to clarify with specificity; to bring a fog over the topic in hand with abstract words and the seeking of generalization where none is possible and none is helpful. The case inquirer should be able to provide and use that specificity and nothing is lost in its refraction through our own understanding as interpreting inquirers: in fact, much is gained as we add a separate viewpoint – one that conjoins and moulds the experiences of others through our own understandings.

Is case study scientific?

The interesting thing about scientists' own reflections on their work and the methodological traditions in which it grew is that there is generally accepted to be no particular, no correct or proper way of generating or marshalling evidence and undertaking inquiry. As Einstein put it, the creative scientist must be an 'unscrupulous opportunist'. The essence of science, he said, is seeking 'in whatever manner is suitable, a simplified and lucid image of the world … There is no logical path, but only intuition' (cited in Holton, 1995: 168).

Some students in the social sciences seem unaware of this methodological eclecticism. In fact, they may assume that 'serious' scientific inquiry is of a different character from case study, and necessarily involves quantification, isolation and manipulation of variables and carefully controlled experiments. This, however, is a product only of a particular kind of late-20th century thinking on research and method. In a classic article about this, two social scientists, Parlett and Hamilton (1972), suggested that social science, and particularly education and psychology, had assumed that the methods of social science should, at their best, properly involve work with large datasets from which generalizations could be made.

Parlett and Hamilton saw this attitude as wrong-headed. They saw the mistake as having emerged from an expropriation by the social sciences of the outlook and methods of certain branches of the biological sciences. In particular, they said, the methods of agricultural scientists and medics had been seen by large sections of the social science establishment as the template within which to fit. They described this outlook, this way of doing social science, as conforming to what they called the *agricultural-botany paradigm*. Agriculturalists do most of their work comparing the growth of fields of wheat or potatoes or soya beans which have been subjected to different treatments. But social scientists cannot, they suggested, treat social analysis in the same way that analysis of the growth of fields of wheat is undertaken.

Their point was that the evaluative methods of agricultural scientists are absolutely appropriate in studying agriculture. But the trouble is that people are not ears of wheat, and nor are they potatoes or even soya beans. We cannot, when we set up social scientific experiments, make assumptions about 'before' and 'after' conditions in the same way that agricultural scientists do, because there aren't befores, middles and afters as there are in fields of crops being dosed with different amounts of fertilizer or insecticide.

People are *agents* in their own destiny (in the way that potatoes are not) and are in the habit of making subtle or even drastic changes to the conditions for a trial. And the measures used to assess change can't be taken with a tape measure or a pair of calipers; they have to be undertaken with test scores, attitude ratings, and so on. The trouble is that the latter are assumed to be of the same order of robustness as the assessments – simple measures of length and weight – that are made of plant growth. But they are not: these social and psychological measures are not the same as centimetres and grammes; they are far less trustworthy. In short, Parlett and Hamilton argued, study undertaken in education and social sciences in this tradition falls short of its own claims to be controlled, exact and unambiguous. (See also Thomas, 2012a.)

We cannot talk about scientific method being licensed by the rigorous use of certain routines and techniques, by procedural ground rules, or even by epistemological premises. Each procedural domain in every science is highly peculiar, depending on its subject's form and texture. From astronomy to physics to zoology, the armoury of the inquirer is unique. Turney (2004) makes the point well in his discussion of Haack's (2003) commentary on the work of scientists:

> Many who think about science for long probably settle somewhere near the view that it is closely akin to other forms of inquiry, albeit with a much more powerful toolkit ... there is nothing special about science, no distinctive scientific method. All empirical inquiry, whether undertaken by a detective, an investigative journalist, an anthropologist in the field or a physicist in the lab, demands the same epistemic virtues. Look for evidence as hard as you can, judge carefully what it is worth, and pay scrupulous attention to what it tells you. Then add this evidence to existing experience and use it to reason out your best-informed conjectures. (Turney, 2004: paras. 1, 3, 4)

Scientific research is, in other words, fluid and multifarious. Assuming otherwise – taking an obstinately monistic view about the procedures characterizing the enterprise of inquiry – leads us on some epistemological wild goose chases.

This point is made commonly in the sociology and philosophy of science. Becker (1998), for example, notes the work of researchers such as Latour and Woolgar (1979) and Lynch (1985), who revealed how natural scientists work 'in ways never mentioned in their formal statements of method, hiding "shop floor practice"' (p. 5). Or, as Medawar (1982) suggests of his own discipline, biology, the special methods and procedures that are supposed to be used by scientists represent merely 'the postures we choose to be seen in when the curtain goes up and the public sees us' (p. 88).

Their message is that the notion of a scientific method is a pretence. We have already noted Einstein's fondness for intuition and his preference for it over method. He went on to explain that 'the whole of science is nothing more than a refinement of everyday thinking' (Einstein, 1936: 351). There is, he was saying, no privileged set of methods in science quarantined away from everyday thinking. We are wrong if we assume that there is some archetypal set of procedures that can collectively be laid over any focus of inquiry that will make our deliberations scientific.

Scientific inquiry is about supplying answers to questions with good evidence and good reasoning, and this can be done in a variety of ways, with the principal feature of importance being the thought and the analysis that goes into providing those answers. We may become over-concerned with the putative shibboleths of science – that is, the things that are taken to be core to the enterprise of science – such as causation and generalization. Einstein's point in the quotation we have just given is that it is not these that are at the core of good scientific thinking. Rather, good inquiry is about making connections and having insights and testing these out, in whatever way. Howard Becker (1998: 41) puts it this way, about how the connections we seek are multi-stranded and multi-directional such that causality is a less-than-helpful concept in social science:

> ... there are many modes of connection, for which we use words like 'influence' or 'causality' or 'dependence'. All these words point to variation. Something will vary and something else, dependent on what happens to the first thing, will undergo some change as well. The things that so vary will often influence each other in complicated ways, so that 'causality' is not really an appropriate way to talk about what we want to emphasize.

Scientific research and the individual case: playing with ideas

In one of his lectures, Schön (1987) made the following point:

> There is ... the notion that the more general and the more theoretical the knowledge, the higher it is. I remember once being quite recently at a school of education, and a graduate student was in a seminar that I was doing, and she was working with nurses, and she said something I thought was interesting. And I asked her if she would give me an example. And she then gave me a proposition which was just as general as the first proposition. So I asked again for an example, and she gave me a proposition which was just slightly less general. And I asked again, and I finally got an example. And I asked her afterwards if she thought it was strange that it took three or four tries to get an example, and she said she *did* think it was strange, and she didn't understand why she'd done that. And I think it is because she had been socialized to an institution where, tacitly and automatically, we believe that the only thing that really counts and the only thing that's really of value is *theory*, and the higher and the more abstract and the more general the theory, the higher the status it is. Under such conditions it's very difficult to give more or less concrete examples. (para. 5)

Pragmatist philosopher John Dewey (1920) expressed the same kind of concern, saying that what was needed was more specific inquiry into a multitude of specific structures and interactions. Both Schön and Dewey were suggesting that inquirers should inhibit a first impulse to make abstract, to generalize, to find principles, to synthesize, and to predict on the basis of that synthesis. The impulse automatically to make abstract constrains our capacity and curtails our desire to research – to look more deeply at – the individual situation and to reflect on that situation. In other words, it leads us away from more valuable ways of thinking about the subjects of our interest. As Wittgenstein warned, the 'craving for generality' and the attendant 'contemptuous attitude toward the particular case' make us 'dismiss as irrelevant the concrete cases which alone could have helped to understand' (1958: 17–20).

Wittgenstein's comments represent a set of counter-positions about inquiry that is, of course, as old as the Athenian hills. The Platonic position, which has a fine and productive record in reductionist science of one kind or another, was that we should look for the *simile in multis* – look, in other words, for the *essence*, the theory, that will capture the truth evinced by many cases. The Aristotelian position, by contrast, was that for many kinds of knowledge we progress only by using our practical reasoning (*phronêsis*), craft knowledge (*technê*), or tacit knowing – the stuff we know because of our experience. It's the stuff we learn 'on the job', and it is explicable and researchable only in terms of the particular context. It cannot therefore be researched via a reduction to general principles (Thomas, 2011a). (Generalization, *phronesis* and *technê* are discussed in detail in Chapters 3 and 4.)

It is the latter, contextual, case-based research on which much applied science should properly focus. We offer two illustrative case studies here about the individual and idiosyncratic process of science and what might be called its *play*. Progress in these instances, and myriad others, rests neither on deliberate attempts to follow scientific method nor on adherence to some set of scientific precepts. Far from it. Rather, progress rests on playing with ideas and the development of an explanatory narrative via the explication of the singular. Here, the work of the scientists is similar to that of educators.

The first case study is from astronomy. In 1967, an astronomical phenomenon (to which the name *pulsar* was later given) was discovered by the astronomer Jocelyn Bell Burnell and her colleagues with the then-new radio telescope at Jodrell Bank near Manchester, England. Her discovery started first with noticing. Doing her routine work, Bell Burnell noticed something unusual. Something in a distant galaxy was giving off massive pulses of radio energy at fantastically regular intervals. This was a mystery, for nothing else in the known universe did anything like this. After the noticing, it was time for conjecture. At first, Bell Burnell and her colleagues conjectured that this was a message from intelligent life: the pulsar was given the name LGM-1 (Little Green Men 1). There was no better explanation for this regular-as-clockwork pulsing. Bell Burnell and her colleagues had to make judgements based on their existing knowledge of phenomena such as this, and one of their first explanatory forays, only half-jokingly, suggested aliens trying to communicate.

But one conjecture was clearly insufficient. To go beyond this, Bell Burnell and her astronomer colleagues began to look in different ways at the pulse. By using their existing knowledge and imaginative speculation – playing with ideas, putting forward and rejecting or accepting plausible hypotheses – they eventually reasoned that these regular pulses were the flashes of radiation from a collapsed neutron star that was spinning at an incredible speed, giving out a directed and extraordinarily condensed beam of radiation, like a lighthouse.

This conclusion was arrived at not through experimental method. The conclusion was drawn by studying just one or two pulsars in a great deal of detail and with a great deal of thinking. Using her own knowledge, the knowledge of the discipline, and the tools of her trade, Bell Burnell drew hugely significant scientific conclusions from this single case.

The second case study is from paleoanthropology. This is how the celebrated paleoanthropologist Louis Leakey described how and why he and his wife, Mary Leakey, started work on hunting for fossils containing evidence about our human forebears in the Olduvai Gorge in Tanzania: 'For some reason both of us had been drawn again and again to this particular site' (Leakey and van Lawick, 1963: 134).

'*For some reason*' says that the reason they started work in this location was beyond their articulable knowledge. It gives a clue about the way that a scientific practitioner tacitly uses evidence – evidence built into something we know as *experience*. For this is what experience is: personal, tacit knowledge built out of information – data, evidence – accumulated both deliberately and fortuitously. Ideas often emerge out of confluences of circumstantial evidence in the minds of those who are steeped in a problem, a practice, a discourse, or a technology, whether we are talking about education, astronomy, or paleoanthropology. Whatever the science, its practitioners swim in the discourse and play with the evidence. Often those scientists have a feeling, a hunch, that this way or that way is the right way to proceed, without being able to articulate its provenance in evidence. There is a playing around with bits and pieces of everyday evidence, bits and pieces of tacit knowledge, that in some way enables practitioners to discover the way to proceed – to conjecture and reason.

Beyond intuiting where to look, the Leakeys played with evidence by collecting fragments of bone and other material and piecing together stories – plausible, intuitively guided accounts – of the way that this pre-human may have led to that one. The evidence they used was not monochromatic. There was knowledge from geology about the age of rocks in which materials were found; there was carbon dating; and there was even knowledge from psychology and physiology. For example, Louis Leakey worked out that one particular pre-human had an ability to use language by looking at the roots of the fossil specimen's teeth: a small depression in the jaw-bone called the canine fossa can be shown to be related to the production of speech, for the little dip makes space for a muscle used in language production (Leakey and van Lawick, 1963). This evidence was acquired through curiosity, serendipity, search, questioning, surprise, and accumulated experience and was melded into a narrative through playing with ideas. It was advanced case study – painstakingly careful examination of the particular. None of this was formally experimental, nor even was there any special method. Yet few would doubt that this case study was science of the most sophisticated kind. From Jocelyn Bell Burnell's pulsar to the Leakeys' fossils, the study was of *cases*.

All scientists – whether physicists, chemists, biologists, paleoanthropologists, or social scientists – use particular kinds of evidence and play with it in particular ways relevant to their fields of work and the methodological traditions that have developed there. But methods are forged around questions; the methods have been the servants, not the executive directors. It is the questions that are important. The natural sciences gained purchase on the world not principally by discovering better methods or by deliberately going out to link theory and practice. On the contrary, they did it by asking good questions – questions germane to the worlds that they studied – and they contrived procedural routes, protean and specialized, to answer these questions. There is no reason not to use case study in answering those questions.

What value is case study?

Much of the discussion around case study research has concerned its value outside the situation of the study itself. What value can there be in case study if we are not able to generalize its findings more widely from the case itself? In answering this question, Stenhouse (1978, 1980) set case study in the context of a discussion of what research *is*, and what it *should be* and he concluded that case study is a basis for generalization via the 'cumulation of data embedded in time'. He proceeded, in response to questions about the usefulness of case study, 'Practice will tend to improve when experience is systematically marshalled as history'.

For Stenhouse, then, it is about the building of knowledge, or theory, from the collation of different forms of case evidence. It is, in other words, the development of an archive of knowledge built from what Berger and Luckmann (1979: 21) have famously called 'multiple realities'. We build exemplary knowledge, making connections between another's experience and our own, seeing links, having insights from the noticed connections. We create what Abbott (1992) calls 'colligations of occurrences'. In discussing the logic of this, Mitchell (2006) concludes that a good deal of the confusion about case study has arisen because of a failure to appreciate that the rationale of extrapolation from a statistical sample to a parent universe involves two very different and even unconnected inferential processes: (i) statistical inference; and (ii) logical or scientific inference; the latter being about the confidence we may have that the logical connection among the features observed in the case relate also to the parent population.

Bassey (1999, 2001) notes that there are two modes of social research: a search for generalities and a study of singularities. He goes on to pick up Simons's (1996) notion of the 'singularity' of the educational situation – that singular status implying everything within the boundary of what is under study. We should, Bassey suggests, actively encourage the descriptive and evaluative study of single events.

In a highly detailed review, Smith (1978) seems in many ways to be in accord with Bassey, but seeks to integrate the latter's arguments with those of Stenhouse and Mitchell. He emerges with interesting points about 'miniature theories' vs. 'general theories'. The study must be framed not in the diluted constructs of generalizing natural science but rather in a kind of 'connective understanding' that comes from any consonance or dissonance which readers of the study may find with their own situations.

In practical terms, this leaves us with a view of case study focusing on local and key phenomena (Thomas, 2012b). Rather than seeking guidance for practice from bodies of theory or generalized knowledge, such study can offer a series of ways of proceeding based in exemplary knowledge. Through such exemplary knowledge, one can make connections between another's experience and one's own, seeing links, having insights.

Conclusion

Case study is about viewing and studying something in its completeness, looking at it from many angles and attempting to understand the interconnectedness of the elements comprising it. To conduct such a study, ways have to be found of taking an over-arching viewpoint. To do this is good science: in fact it is the essence of good science. Although we cannot generalize from case study, generalization is not always what is wanted from inquiry: we don't always want or need generalization, and some of the most inspired and insightful research, of any kind, has come about from case study. What case study is especially good for is getting a rich picture and gaining analytical insights about it. The 'analytical' part of this is the key element: each study has a subject of interest (a person, place, event or phenomenon) and an analytical frame within which it is studied. The subject of interest is the lens through which we can examine the theoretical topic of interest.

We shall examine the important distinction between the subject of interest and the theoretical topic of interest further in Chapter 5. Before that, though, in the next two chapters we need to look at the provenance and history of case inquiry and some concepts important to understanding its anatomy.

TWO

The history of case study and its epistemological status

The case study has its roots in work done in many and varied disciplines. As Garvin (2003) notes, it was a lawyer who had, in 1870, named case study method, and his concern was principally for the use of the case study in university teaching. The case had begun to be used, though, around the same time and a little before, in explicating and analyzing social and psychological phenomena. At the beginning of the 19th century, Jean-Marc-Gaspard Itard described his now-celebrated work with Victor, the 'wild boy of Aveyron', and later in the century Frédéric Le Play made his highly influential studies of French working people (see Mogey, 1955).

The aims of these latter analysts lay not in teaching. Rather, there was systematic reporting and theorizing about a particular person or set of people. Analysis based on this kind of work began to chime, at the beginning of the 20th century, with new thought about social inquiry and how it should be undertaken. It resonated with new ideas about interpretative inquiry, encapsulated in symbolic interactionism, in such a way that it became a force in and of itself. The case study, exemplified in, for example, Thomas and Znaniecki's (1958 [1927]) iconic explication of the life of American immigrants, *The Polish Peasant in Europe and America*, became an accepted and respected form of research.

The case study presents a view of inquiry that takes a pragmatic view of knowledge – one that elevates a view of life in its complexity. It's the realization that complexity in social affairs is often indivisible which has led to case study's status as one of the most popular and most fertile design frames open to the researcher, and this is perhaps the reason behind its popularity among researchers in the social sciences. Here, it seems particularly apposite that the richness of the living tapestries being studied is acknowledged and employed by the methods of inquiry used to research into them.

Recognizing complexity and looking at the whole represents something of a new worldview. It is one that has emerged during the 20th century with the aim of understanding people and events not as phenomena comprising disparate disconnected parts but rather as phenomena with interconnected elements interplaying in a kind of social ecology. Anyone wanting to do case study implicitly shares this worldview, though it should be said that case study does not boast an intellectual allegiance to any one strand of thought but rather to many. We will review some of these in this chapter.

To break things down or to see them as wholes?

Given that case study is not attached to one school of thought it may seem something of an intellectual orphan, and this is part of its problem in attempting to establish its credibility. But while it may not adhere to a particular stream of thought or school of thinking, its emphasis on the whole – the holistic – puts it in some respected scholarly company. All of this company shares a wish to see and understand things as wholes.

But the wish to see things more as wholes presents a number of challenges since the thrust of most scientific inquiry since the Enlightenment (i.e. since the beginnings of rational and scientific thought in the mid-17th century) has been about breaking things down. It has been about reducing them and understanding phenomena in terms of their constituent parts. It has, in other words, been about reduction, and this is known to philosophers as *reductionism*. Reductionism has procured great achievements in the natural sciences and the technology that springs from it: people on the Moon; refrigeration; antibiotics; computers, and so on. Viewing the world from this position, phenomena are nothing more than the sum of their parts. The starting point taken in case study, by contrast, is that certain phenomena are *more* than the sum of their parts and have to be understood as a whole, rather than as a set of inter-relating variables. How has this holistic position fared next to the super-successful reductionism? And given that reductionism has been so successful, why would anyone want to study things differently?

This chapter is really about the attempt to view and analyze phenomena as *more* than the sum of their parts and about the intellectual traditions, mainly in the 20th century rather than before, that have competed against the highly productive reductionist tradition. This has, of course, been a bit of a David vs. Goliath contest. There are a number of themed but unrelated elements to this understanding of things-as-a-whole that we shall look at briefly, each in its own different way about the importance of wholeness in inquiry.

The issue is more complex than simply seeing the world as indivisibly complete *versus* the world as necessarily divisible and reducible. Associated with the assumptions being made here are beliefs about the purpose of inquiry. In other words, why are we doing the research? Some have said that the purpose of research is to develop laws and theories with which we can explain the world and predict what is likely to happen next. Others have said that this may be a perfectly satisfactory way of going about things in understanding the phenomena of the natural sciences, but it is inadequate to understand the things of the social world. Here, reductionism is of less value.

The issue about whether reductionism is of value had its origins in Athens: Plato, Socrates and Aristotle had major disagreements about this. Plato and Socrates averred that universal truths developed from generalization are what we should all be searching for if we want true knowledge. They looked for, in other words, the *essence*, the theory, the *simile in multis* which will capture the truth evinced by many cases.

Aristotle disagreed on the value of *simile in multis*. For many kinds of knowledge, says Aristotle, we progress only by using our practical reasoning, craft knowledge, or tacit knowing – the stuff we know because of our experience. It's the stuff we learn 'on the job', or by simply being alive and it is explicable only in terms of the particular: the case. It cannot be communicated by reducing it down to general principles. He suggested that it was wrong to dismiss the value of cases in the production of knowledge. We explore this further in Chapter 3.

The controversy on this theme continues to the present day. It proceeded through the Renaissance, with Francis Bacon, the first scientist, some would say, averring that the generalizers and regularizers, the followers of Plato, '... hasted to their theories and dogmaticals, and were imperious and scornful toward particulars'. Today, the argument has unfortunately come to be known as 'paradigm wars' (see Oakley, 1999), and shows little sign of abating.

It was those who argued for the *simile in multis* whose ideas won (broadly speaking) and whose thinking took hold so successfully for the natural sciences. This was a big loss for our ways of understanding, asserts an astute commentator on these issues, Bent Flyvbjerg (2001). Flyvbjerg says that the mistake led humankind on two millennia of false starts in understanding social phenomena. The mistake was in the failure to distinguish between different kinds of inquiry for different purposes and it leads us, in extremis, to the absurd position that it is inappropriate to argue or learn from particular examples, for fear that this might be thought 'anecdotal' and, therefore, unscientific.

The distinction, then, has been on a long journey intellectually. In essence it is about the relevance of particular, individual events to a larger picture, and the extent to which we can use separate events in establishing laws or theories by which we can explain and predict. Some say that it is legitimate to generalize in the natural sciences but not in the social sciences. In the former, physics and chemistry, the stability of the events studied is such that laws and theories can be worked out in such a way that they will prove useful for explanation and prediction. In the human sciences, however, events follow such random twists and turns that any attempt at establishing stable laws and theories that will reliably explain and predict is meaningless. The classic argument here has been posed by Alasdair MacIntyre (1985) in his book *After Virtue*.

We have noted that this argument about reductionism versus holism has been going on for 2,500 years and that reductionism has certainly won as far as method for the natural sciences is concerned. In fact, it's only in the last hundred years or so that protagonists of Aristotle's views have come to the fore again in thinking about the human sciences. It is worth looking here at the idea of the ideograph, which is a drawing or figure that stands not for a sound, as in the Roman alphabet, but for an idea, from the Greek word *'idea'* meaning (unsurprisingly) 'idea' or 'private', and *gramma* meaning 'drawing'. It was the philosopher Wilhelm Windelband who, at the cusp of the 19th and 20th centuries, drew on the notion of the ideograph to separate what he called the 'idiographic' and the 'nomothetic' (from the Greek *nomos* meaning 'law') in social inquiry.

With the idiographic, the approach is to specify and to study individual phenomena in detail: we have a 'picture' in front of us. With the nomothetic, by contrast, the approach is to generalize from many cases and to derive laws from such generalization.

Windelband was not the first to comment on the difference between the idiographic and the nomothetic but – as is so often the case in the history of ideas – he encapsulated something nicely in his separation of the one from the other and the distinction he drew has stuck: it has proved enormously helpful in summarizing the differences between these kinds of inquiry.

Gestalt psychology

Not long after Windelband, one interesting avenue down which this discussion travelled was that of *Gestalt* psychology early in the 20th century. This was key for case study since the essence of Gestalt thinking is that things should be seen in their totality, as we try to do in case study. The key idea to emerge here was that the mind works not by seeing things in isolation, separately, but rather as wholes – as integrated units. We humans, alone amongst animals, invest meaning in what appear to be unrelated phenomena and we make patterns, make sense, out of these. It is almost as if our minds are pattern-making or sense-making machines.

The key figures here – psychologists such as Max Wertheimer and Wolfgang Köhler (and, later, the social psychologist Kurt Lewin, the architect of action research) – suggested that the methods psychologists use to study psychological phenomena distort our understanding of them. By always reducing, atomizing the subject matter of psychology into constituent variables, the end result is a misunderstanding of the way the mind works, they said. The mind is best understood not by using the convenient building blocks of psychological science – variables such as gender, age, reaction speed, time, class – but rather by looking at the way in which it deals with phenomena in their wholeness.

It is certainly true that *Homo Sapiens* is a pattern-finding animal: the fertility of our brains in divining patterns is boundless. It requires only the mildest encourage-ment for shape and form to crystallize out of what may seem at first to be chaotic stimuli. In fact, perhaps dangerously for certain kinds of inquiry, we even seem to be predisposed to see form where there is none, rather than not to see form. The phi-losopher Karl Popper (1977: 270) suggested that this faculty may be inborn; it may be due, he proposed, to 'mechanisms which make us search for regularities' and may be responsible for what he called 'the dogmatic way of thinking'. In a similar vein, Barrow (1997) points out that the human brain has an evolutionary imperative to *over*see patterns: the occasional seeing of patterns where they did not exist (as 'false positives' – for instance, 'seeing' regular slender shadows as tiger stripes) would have an evolutionary advantage over the non-recognition of patterns where they in fact did exist (the actual stripes of the tiger). In other words, we must be cautious about this precious ability to see pattern since we may harbour a predilection to make shape and theory out of that which is shapeless.

We may, in other words, overplay generalization: we may tend to generalize from insufficient information. It is this tendency that has to be guarded against in all of the sampling procedures that have been developed with what has been called probabilistic research. But if we are looking at ideographs (that is, cases) rather than representative samples, we are not expecting to generalize. Rather, we are expecting to employ to best effect our ready-made strengths in making sense *without* generali-zation. Generalization may not be possible from case study. However, what inquirers can do is to use their ability to put things together, to draw from experience, to make informed judgements about cause and effect in a particular case.

Dramas, theatres and stages

Seeing the person in context – where the action is defined by interactions among people and situations – is, of course, the *sine qua non* of case study research. Each person is affected by the environment around them: no one is an island. To under-stand the dynamics of these contexts it is useful to see the social world rather as a stage on which the social actors play roles depending on the dramas they are enacting. Sociologist Erving Goffman called this view of social life *dramaturgy*. In the dictionary definition, 'dramaturgy' is the art of writing and producing plays. And, for Goffman, life is a set of dramatic performances where people take on roles and change the way they behave depending on their interactions with other actors. Goffman differentiated between the kinds of situations in which such performances are necessary, noting that there is a 'front stage' where the 'act' is always used in order to 'impression-manage', and a backstage where people can be more 'themselves'.

Goffman's dramaturgical perspective was itself an offshoot, an important one, of a branch of sociology known as symbolic interactionism. Herbert Blumer (1992), one of symbolic interactionism's main proponents, presents what he calls the 'basic premises' and 'methodological consequences' of this school of sociology as follows:

> ... human beings interpret or 'define' each other's actions instead of merely reacting to each other's actions. Their 'response' is not made directly to the actions of one another but instead is based on the meaning which they attach to such actions. Thus, human interaction is mediated by the use of symbols, by interpretation, or by ascertaining the meaning of one another's actions. (1992: 82)

Symbolic interactionism is in turn a tributary of *interpretivism*. The basic assumption here is that the social world is *constructed* by each of us differently, with words and events carrying different meanings for each person and in each situation. Interpretivism started, broadly speaking, with the American sociologist George Herbert Mead.

Though not directly linked, a forerunner to these lines of thought was the phenomenology of Edmund Husserl, which emerged at the beginning of the 20th century. This is generally thought of as a philosophical rather than a sociological movement, but it is connected to the thinking of the interpretivists and the symbolic interactionists in its emphasis on meanings. Actions, Husserl averred, cannot be broken down into their constituent elements to understand them (see Welton, 1999). They are understandable only in terms of the meanings that actors impose on them. They are understandable only, in other words, in terms of the wholeness of the context in which they occur.

In fact, a clutch of philosophers, and those in the infant disciplines of sociology and psychology, were saying much the same kind of thing at this time. Wilhelm Dilthey came up with the idea of *verstehen* (meaning 'understanding'), more adequately to demarcate between the stuff of the natural and the human sciences and our ways of inquiring into them. We cannot, he said, ignore the historical context and the context of meaning in all that human beings do and say (see Makkreel and Rodi, 1991).

Ecological psychology

Another manifestation of the need for wholeness is seen in ecological psychology. Usually, the word 'ecology' refers to the relationships between living things in the environments that they inhabit. It is the study of the complex interrelationships that take place in those environments. A starting point here is that the lives of organisms that inhabit these environments are inextricably intertwined with the nature and quality of those environments. Changes in any small aspect of the environment will have knock-on effects which will affect the lives of the organisms that populate it. An important aspect of this is that there will be an equilibrium in this environment and this equilibrium will be maintained. The same phenomenon of maintenance occurs in the environments (family, school, workplace, etc.) that we inhabit as people.

So, ecological psychologists would say, people – human beings – live in a multi-coloured world. It's an ecology, where an increase in one stimulus invokes not an automatic reflex or a tropism but a thought-out reaction. For example, ecological psychologists would say that one could not set up a meaningful research study to assess the effect of turning up the music volume in a room on people's conversation volume. Of course, it could be done, physically: some volunteers could be asked to converse in a room where rock music is playing quietly while the volume was increased; simultaneously, the volunteers' voice volume could be measured. One would expect to find that the volunteers' voice levels rose. (Much psychological experimentation is of this kind.) But, an ecological psychologist would say, the real world is not like this. In the real world people would just leave the room to talk, or someone would go and turn the volume down again – then someone would go and turn it up again, then perhaps there would be an argument, and so on. The real world is complex, and it is the real world in which we are interested. The understanding that ecological psychology offered was that the way people behaved in the psychological laboratory with its tight control of a small number of variables does not remotely represent the way that people behave in the real world.

The basic idea is the same as the one behind symbolic interactionism: it is that no behaviour occurs in a vacuum; it occurs in the context of others' activity, in the context of the family, place of work or school or community and the context of the linguistic, cultural, legal and physical environments. Because of the way that psychology and its inquiries typically proceed, by isolating variables, controlling important ones, and manipulating one or two, we can get into a rut of thinking that our inquiries using these controls and manipulations are valid representations of what happens in our everyday lives. We come to think of the world in which we live as being really like this – like a psychological laboratory with a simple set of variables that are all more or less inert in their relationships with one another.

The traditional focus on the individual in psychological endeavour permeates the applied field, where interventions also often take place in a vacuum, with scant consideration of the physical and social environments within which individuals learn and behave. The ecological metaphor used by some psychologists since the mid-20th century enables an understanding that things are not that simple. Within an environment, behaviours may emerge which are a consequence of conditions outside the narrow ambit of the individual. Changing one or two features of this system may have unanticipated consequences, or may have no effect at all.

Taking an ecological model is like using a wide-angle lens, enabling an examination of the wider situation which surrounds the target, and encouraging analysis in that wider situation. In essence, an ecological view enables a recognition that people inhabit a variety of contexts, each one impinging upon the other. Any attempt to over-simplify the richness of the ways in which these contexts interplay is bound to have shortcomings. An ecological view recognizes that it is impossible to disentangle the functioning of a constellation of phenomena simultaneously interrelating in any social arena.

Barker (1968) suggested that behaviour settings have both static and dynamic attributes. On the static side, the setting consists of one or more standing patterns of behaviour-and-milieu, the latter comprising elements such as house, classroom, a windy day. On the dynamic side, the setting comprises the interpersonal relationships among people and groups. Some forms of supposedly scientific inquiry, Barker says, attempt to keep apart the static and the dynamic, the physical and the behavioural. But their interaction is the centre-point of his attention; he gives the name *synomorphs* to the settings in which these interactions occur.

Amidst Barker's complex analysis is a continual reiteration of the influence of the physical environment and its interaction with a range of other influences such as the ideologies of the participants, and the procedures, practices or rituals associated with certain 'synomorphs'. It is notable that Barker and others such as Bateson (1999 [1972]), who promoted an ecological thrust to understanding people in their environments, themselves had a multidisciplinary scholarly background and promoted intellectual interchange among different fields.

Another important figure in an ecological framing of psychology is Kurt Lewin, who developed 'field theory' (Lewin (2008 [1946]). Lewin suggested the 'field' of an individual's psyche comprised a range of social and psychological factors and changes with a person's experience. An alternative term he uses for fields is 'lifespaces' – home, job, school, sports club, etc. – which we occupy at different times and in different ways. All are joined by 'vectors' that operate at different levels of strength.

Systems thinking

Systems thinking is a way of viewing the world that lends itself naturally to case study since it aims to see the system as a whole. The difference is that systems theory and its various branches are bounded by some quite firm frameworks about viewing the interrelationships that exist. With case study there are no methodological prescriptions. By contrast, systems theory proffers methodological tools and route maps to assist analysis. It's a *particular* way of studying the whole, unlike case study. This is not to say that you cannot use the methods of systems thinking *in* a case study.

Systems theory was developed in a variety of contexts from biology to engineering, and thus can be relevant for a range of foci and can be adapted for use in each of these. If your interests are in engineering or biology or in an applied science, or if you are interested in the interrelationship between one of these and the social world, it may well be worth exploring aspects of systems theory. The models for understanding that have been advanced in systems thinking were developed specifically to address the need for holism in understanding complex dynamics. As with the parallel trains of thought in psychology and sociology that we have just looked at, the finger is pointed at the barrenness of attempts to understand complex behaviour by reductionist methods. Our understanding, systems theorists say, has to push that complexity to the front: we have to try to understand the ability of the complex system to adapt, change and learn from experience. Systems theory used ideas from biology such as *negative entropy* (or the ability of a system to make sense, re-form itself and maintain an equilibrium) and from mechanics, such as *feedback* (the effect of a signal going back into a loop and magnifying itself each time it returns). These are characteristics of systems that are not seen in individual parts of the system.

One of the first proponents of systems theory was Ludwig von Bertalanffy (1950) with his *General Systems Theory*. The same theme emerges: one of complex inter-actions, though von Bertalanffy made an important distinction between what he called open systems and closed systems. A closed system will be one such as an engineering system (e.g. an internal combustion engine), which has very little in the way of a change to its movement once it is working, aside perhaps from a movement of the throttle by the operator. By contrast, an open system is one such as a biological system (e.g. any living thing, even a bacterium), which seeks to maintain itself in equilibrium by responding to its environment. Apart from features such as feedback and negative entropy, von Bertalanffy spoke about features such as *isomorphism* (i.e. being the same shape) between biological and social systems – so a beehive could be seen as having similarities to a town.

His thinking led naturally to interdisciplinarity, with insights from one field providing clues for thinking about how things work in another. In fact, von Bertalanffy expected to see more of an integration of the work of science – natural and social. He said that the human sciences were too often atomistic, that they were a kind of 'social physics' of the worst kind.

Beyond all of this, systems theory has been taken forward by others in some interesting ways that may be quite useful to the case researcher. One of these is in the development of 'soft systems theory', expounded by Checkland (1981) and his colleagues at Lancaster University. Checkland tried to incorporate the basic tenets of systems thinking while offering a framework for seeing the ways that the elements interconnect. Developing his 'soft systems' within the context of industrial psychology, he suggested that the matters with which applied social scientists are concerned are complex wholes which maintain themselves in a changing environment. They do this through adaptation and control action.

Although the concepts used in Checkland's model are borrowed from biology and engineering, he does not explicitly use the ecological metaphor. However, his aims are congruent with those of the ecological psychologists. He suggests a model which draws a distinction between the 'real world' and 'systems thinking' and forces an analysis of both. He asserts that the 'soft, messy problems of human beings in their everyday lives' are not amenable to the methods of the 'hard' systems tradition of engineering. He suggests that the hard systems tradition can handle natural (that is, biological) systems and designed systems (such as bicycles, computers, mathematics) but cannot cope in situations dominated by human perceptions. He calls the latter human activity systems.

His soft systems method suggests the following sequence of events and processes. First, a statement is made of the situation in which there is perceived to be a problem; each social situation is taken to be an interacting system of roles, norms and values. Second, an analysis is made of the problem. This involves drawing a 'rich picture' of the situation, in which the relationship of structure and process is noted. At this stage themes are extracted and these themes represent statements about the situation which the analyst regards as puzzling, problematic, interesting or significant. This analysis has so far been at the real-world level. But at the third stage the researcher descends into soft systems thinking. Here, the analyst identifies systems operating in the situation and their function in that situation. It is here that an analogy with the ecosystem is clearest. The aim is to identify from the 'rich picture' the functions of behaviours and sets of behaviours within the situation. Checkland gives the name 'relevant systems' to these. From these relevant systems a 'root definition' is arrived at, which essentially describes the analyst's view of the problem situation on the basis of the posited relevant systems. The fourth stage involves the construction of 'conceptual models' of the systems isolated in stage 3. The final stages involve a journey back into the 'real world' and a comparison of these models with what exists in the real world.

Ecological systems theory

Urie Bronfenbrenner's (1979) work is interesting as a fusion of ecological psychology and systems thinking. Being a psychologist rather than a sociologist, Bronfenbrenner did not share the sociologist's fondness for theatres and stages as metaphors. Rather than seeing human behaviour and activity as a drama, he saw it as an ecology. The metaphor was biological rather than theatrical.

Bronfenbrenner has perhaps contributed most systematically to furthering the ways in which the ecological approach can be used practically. It was he who could also be said to have been the most assertive proponent of ecological approaches, with some quite direct attacks on the more narrowly scientific approaches to psychology of his contemporaries. For him, a parallel track was not sufficient. He saw psychology's traditional methods actually doing harm to an understanding of people and he wanted to force a reappraisal of its traditions, habits and methods. It could almost be said that Bronfenbrenner was aiming for a paradigm shift in the way that psychology proceeded as a form of science.

For him, culture and society provide a set of 'instructions' for how social settings are made and he integrated discussion of context into a formal framework which he developed as a form of 'systems theory' (and see Bronfenbrenner and Morris, 1998). He saw ecological environments as being composed of micro-, meso-, exo- and macrosystems. A microsystem is a pattern of activities, roles and interpersonal relations of an individual in a given setting. A mesosystem is a system of microsystems. An exosystem is a setting where the individual is not involved but where events occur that affect or are affected by the individual's setting. A macrosystem comprises the belief systems or ideology that structure other, lower systems (see Figure 2.1).

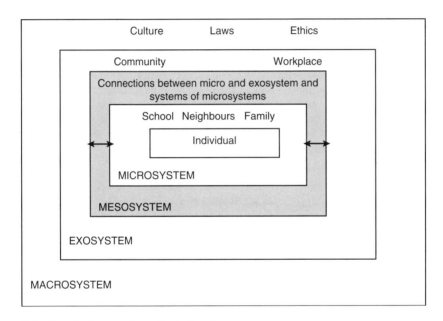

Figure 2.1   Bronfenbrenner's ecological systems

So, taking an ecological and Bronfenbrenner-type view, if – to take an example – Samantha decides not to get up and go to work today how can we explain this? Looking just in one-dimensional terms we might see it in terms of depression. But looking more widely, we might see it in terms of friendships, and Sam's lack of contacts, having just emigrated from Australia. Looking out even more widely we might find a problem that she has been having at work. Even more broadly, she may be affected by an overdue tax return and a demand to her employers from the tax authorities to take tax directly from her salary.

Such an understanding is far distant conceptually and analytically from traditional psychological inquiry and is now encouraged by a new wave of clinical psychologists such as David Smail. Indeed, in what sounds like an echo of Bronfenbrenner, Smail (1993: 13) asserts that 'There is certainly no evidence that the wider availability of psychological theories and techniques is leading to a decrease in psychological distress'. It is the over-simplifying models that are used for human psychology and distress that are to blame, says Smail.

Thinking particularly about children, Bronfenbrenner's comment on traditional psychological inquiry was that it sacrificed far too much to gain experimental control and led to 'the science of strange behaviour of children in strange situations with strange adults for the briefest possible periods of time' (1979: 19). The links with symbolic interactionism are manifest.

Conclusion

The stress on the context and the 'wholeness' of behaviour is many-stranded and is particularly suited to case study, with its emphasis on the holistic. Arguments underlining the need to look at the whole picture have a long intellectual history. Figure 2.2 summarizes some of the schools of thought – finding their origins in psychological, sociological and philosophical traditions – that have led to today's more eclectic attitude to inquiry. It's an attitude that accepts the relevance and utility of the idiographic and provides ways of addressing wholeness by emphasizing rather than denying the interconnectedness of the strands of psychological and social life.

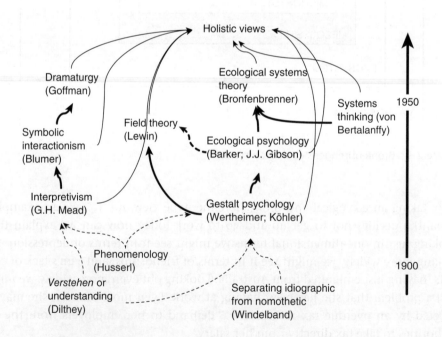

Figure 2.2 Holism and its schools of thought

THREE

Generalization, phronesis and the case study

Although case study may take many forms, its essence is defined by Stake (1995: xi) as 'the study of the particularity and complexity of a single case, coming to understand its activity within important circumstances'. Stake's definition provides a good starting point for this chapter, stressing as it does the particularity of the idiographic, for it is this very particularity that has been troubling for case study. The following quotations make the point:

> The case study has long been (and continues to be) stereotyped as a weak sibling among social science methods. (Yin, 2003: xiii)

> 'You cannot generalize from a single case,' some [colleagues] would say, 'and social science is about generalizing'. Flyvbjerg (2006: 219)

> Case histories are a laborious approach to understanding. For situations are so varied that even a large number of cases may be a misleading sample ... and none is comprehensible outside the historical sequence in which it grew. (Vickers, 1965: 173)

Here, three social scientists sum up what might be called the standard social scientific view on cases and case study. Yin points to case study's low status; Flyvbjerg (in his summary of colleagues' comments) and Vickers suggest reasons for that status, principally in the paucity of general understanding offered by case study. It is *general* understanding that is the key, and *generality* goes to the heart of the matter, for it is here, in generality or universals that we find issues of what social science, and particularly theory in social science, has distinctively to offer. Theory in social science often appears to materialize in the search for regularity and order in the general, and the nature of the regularity on offer is what distinguishes the putatively special contribution of the social scientist from the common-or-garden insight of the lay-person. It provides the 'warrant' for the claims of the research. The construction of *generalized* and *generalizable* knowledge of a particular quality is the cynosure of the social scientist.

This emphasis on generalized knowledge is a problem for case study, which offers little in the way of generalizable information. From experiment to ethnography, it is generalizing and generalization that hold appeal for social scientists. In experiment, the use of sampling and inferential statistics concerns the degree to which general conclusions can be drawn from particular circumstances: there is even a special term to describe the extent to which such conclusions can be drawn: 'external validity' (Campbell, 1957). And in ethnography, Becker (1998) talks of his tutor Everett C. Hughes, who suggested that 'theorizing' consisted of 'a collection of *generalizing tricks* he used to think about society' (1998: 3, emphasis added). Althusser (1979: 183–90) sees something similar in all scientific process: it all involves some generalizing from the knowledge generated in the course of ordinary activity to the level of scientific theory. In this regard, he distinguishes between different kinds of generality: I, II and III. For Althusser, generalizing proceeds from the raw material generality of I, worked on by the 'means of production' constructs of Generalities II to produce the working knowledge of Generalities III. Seen in this way, generalization is the inescapable ingredient of scientific process, but operates at differing levels in the crystallization of ideas. Likewise, for Nadel (1957: 1–2) generalization is at the core of 'theorization': he talks of theory consisting of interconnected generalizations existing in such a way that 'observable consequences logically follow'.

This imperative to understand at the level of the universal, the general, involves the distillation of understanding to some principle – or to something rather weaker, such as one of Hughes's 'generalizing tricks'. Its centrality is at the core of argument against the validity of case study method. However, an argument can be made that case study is not alone in its shortcomings on the generalizability front, and if this argument is valid the particular critiques of case study amongst method in social science may be misplaced.

MacIntyre (1985: 88) had an important point to make about the larger issue on generalization in the social sciences. He put it this way: '... the salient fact about those [social] sciences is the absence of the discovery of any law-like generalizations whatsoever'. It may be, in other words, that any generalizations with which social scientists emerge are no better than those that emerge from, for example, the 'common interpretive acts' spoken about by Schatzman (1991) – the Generalities I of Althusser. What, then, is the offer of the social scientist over and above the offer of the lay-person? How does the social scientist's contribution bestow any distinctiveness over what might be called 'everyday generalization'? One of the authors has discussed this elsewhere (Thomas, 2002).

As a part of an attempt to understand the provenance of the reasoning that underpins resistance to case study, it is the purpose of this chapter to look at the claim of social science to discover a special kind of generalizable knowledge. We look also at why social science should want to do this.

The important consequence for the use of case study in social science is in that which is lost if there is always a spoken or unspoken recourse to generality – whether this is expressed overtly or whether it emerges through reference to theory. The corollary is in the way that the knowledge proffered from case study is taken to be understood. Is it taken to be understood as generalizable in the context of theory, as in the traditional model of natural science, or is it seen as corrigible and interpretable in the context of experience – in the context of phronesis?

Case study and generality: *simile in multis*

There is the same degree of licentiousness and error in forming axioms, as in abstracting notions: and that in the first principles, which depend on common induction. (Francis Bacon, 1854 [1620]: 345)

Drawing from textbook and reference book definitions of case study, Flyvbjerg (2001) concludes that the case study remains in an unusual place, somewhere outside the canon of respectable social scientific method. The reason for this, he implies, lies in atavistic tensions over the nature of science. While such tensions have been superseded by more eclectic reasoning in the natural sciences themselves – where there is no question about the validity of the specific case as a source of information and analysis – they still have valency in the social sciences. In the latter, the pursuit of scientific truth is taken to be vitiated by the inherent unreliability and unreplicability of the singular case. This tension, suggests Flyvbjerg, rests in a false contradiction about the goals of the human sciences.

We began to discuss this tension in Chapter 2, but it is worth pursuing its provenance in more detail. While Aristotle emphasized the significance of case knowledge, Socrates and Plato dismissed the value of cases in the production of knowledge. Socrates would, in the dialogues (Plato, 2004: 63), always seek general definitions, responding dismissively to his discussants about the concrete examples they would offer: 'Do you not understand that I am looking for the *"simile in multis"'*. But Aristotle, Plato's pupil, insisted that one cannot be satisfied with universals and that knowledge is validly conceived of as *phronesis* – or, in today's terms, practical reasoning, craft knowledge, or tacit knowing: the ability to see the right thing to do in the circumstances. Carr and Kemmis (1986) usefully discuss phronesis in the context of teacher development, and Grundy (1987: 61) offers a helpful explication, giving a view of phronesis that involves knowledge about what is 'fitting' on a particular occasion. She suggests that phronesis involves a combination of knowledge, judgement and 'taste', together producing a 'discernment' which is more than a mere skill. This kind of practical reasoning and judgement, we shall argue presently, is best explicable in terms of the particular: the case.

But as Plato's thinking took hold so successfully for the natural sciences, Aristotle's, located in the *phronesis* of human learning and behaviour, was largely disregarded. This mistake, asserts Flyvbjerg (2001), has led us to two millennia of false starts in understanding social phenomena.

The mistake was in the failure to distinguish between different kinds of inquiry for different purposes and it leads us, in extremis, to the absurd position that it is inappropriate to argue, gain insight or learn from particular examples, for fear that this might be thought anecdotal and, ergo, unscientific. The consequences radiate into all potential forms of commentary and analysis, and manifest themselves in the thinking of professional researcher and student alike.

The problem is in the seeking of the general as part of the assumption that generalizable knowledge is in some way to be privileged over exemplary knowledge. The distinction we make in this chapter is between generalizable knowledge and its association with theory on the one side, and exemplary knowledge and its location in phronesis on the other. We shall define and discuss each as we proceed, but first we must look more closely at generalization and the expectations surrounding it.

What is generalization in social science and what is expected of it?

Bassey (2001) notes the ways that commentators have tried to deal with variabilities in understanding the generalizing enterprise:

> Perhaps Yin's concept of an 'analytic generalization' is very similar to Stenhouse's 'retrospective generalization', Erickson's 'assertion' and Stake's 'propositional generalization'. ... Perhaps Tripp's 'qualitative generalization' is akin to Stake's 'naturalistic generalization'. But to draw such comparisons is a dangerous game for I cannot be sure that I have correctly elicited what these writers have meant by the terms they have used and, dare I say it, neither can we be sure that these writers themselves had clear, unambiguous concepts in their minds and managed to express them coherently. (Bassey, 2001: 6)

Bassey does a useful service in reviewing the disconnected and idiosyncratic vocabulary of generalization in social science (though he misses the 'holographic generalization' of Lincoln and Guba (1985)). In reviewing it he also points to precisely the dangers of social scientific generalization raised by MacIntyre. In other words, if we cannot determine the 'error bars' associated with a generalization, we are left with, at best, an everyday generalization. (Bassey's solution was to try to *establish* these 'error bars', and we shall come to this in a moment.)

MacIntyre had suggested that social science's generalizations are no better than everyday generalizations because they lack not only universal quantifiers, but also scope modifiers, that is to say 'they are not only not genuinely of the form "For all *x* and some *y* if *x* has property ϕ, then *y* has property ψ," but we cannot say of them in any precise way under what conditions they hold' (MacIntyre, 1985: 91). He goes on to note that the standard reasoning behind the relationship between explanation and prediction is that *explanation* involves the invocation of a law-like generalization *retro*spectively, while *prediction* involves the invocation of a similar generalization *pro*spectively – and the diminution of predictive failure is the mark of progress in science. He suggests there has been no diminution of predictive failure in the social 'sciences': there has been no progress. Examining both the unpredictable and predictable elements, he proceeds to assert that in the relationship between the two, unpredictability will always win over predictability as far as the matters of social science are concerned. It is only the trivial things that are predictable, and we don't need any kind of sophisticated social 'science' to tell us about these. Some years later, Wrong (2003) put it this way:

> A major legitimation of the science-building project in the social sciences used to be to insist on the predictability of human behavior ... It was pointed out triumphantly that people wear similar clothes, eat at specific times of the day, observe common rules of grammar in speaking, drive on the same side of the road and stop at red lights ... Yet it was overlooked that the successful 'prediction' of none of these regularities depends on systematic inquiry by a group of specialists claiming to apply methods to the study of human life in society that have proven astoundingly successful in the natural sciences. (2003: 141–2)

In short, what can usefully be generalized about in social 'science' can only be 'uninteresting' or mundane – concerning everyday generalization. In her novel *Under the Net,* Iris Murdoch puts it well in the words of Annandine:

> If by expressing a theory you mean that someone else could make a theory about what you do, of course that is true and uninteresting ... But then all sorts of obvious lies and fantasies may be part of such a situation; and you would say that one must be good at detecting and shunning lies, and not that one must be good at lying. (2002: 91)

What characterizes the interesting, as distinct from the 'uninteresting' of Murdoch, in the subjects of social science is 'pervasive unpredictability'. This renders all projection in social life 'permanently vulnerable and fragile' (MacIntyre, 1985: 103), and we would add that it also corrodes any possibility of *special* retrospective generalization (that is to say, concerned with explanation rather than prediction). Stake (1978) makes the same point, noting that inappropriate generalization fosters misunderstanding. What we have to do, if we are persuaded by MacIntyre's critique, is to be sure that the 'lies and fantasies' promulgated by everyday generalization are not given a sheen of scientific respectability by the pretence of special generalization.

If social scientific generalizations offer nothing special, are we left with the conclusion that the generalizations of social scientists can in fact be no better than their competitors in everyday guesses and assumptions, homily, proverbs and maxims? 'No: let's not minimize our offer', social scientists have sometimes countered: we can say that we are left with probabilistic generalizations enhanced via some process of assessment wherein the probability of a finding is calibrated. This is the line that

Bassey (2001: 7) takes in his promotion of 'fuzzy generalization' specifically in education: it should be accompanied by a 'best estimate of trustworthiness' (BET), says Bassey (2001: 19). This BET should be based on researchers' own insights, so that they might be able to say that an outcome is likely to happen a particular proportion of the time, which they might express as a BET of a particular percentage.

It is difficult to agree with Bassey that this provides 'a solution to the problem of generalization in educational research'. The problem is that if the calculation of such an important qualifier is to be based on the experience and insight of the researcher, one wonders why empirical research should be needed at all. If the researchers' experiences and insights are to be afforded such significance in the analysis of findings, why should one not proceed in formulating policy and advice about social phenomena solely on the basis of researchers' accumulated knowledge and experience?

One has to return to the status of social scientific generalization vis-à-vis generalization in the natural sciences. Hammersley (2001: 220) suggests that *all* such generalizations should be seen as 'cautious formulations' with no clear distinctions to be made between natural scientific and other endeavour (a point similar to one made by Lincoln and Guba (1985), who go so far as to draw on Hofstadter's discussion of Gödel's theorem, which states that all consistent axiomatic formulations of number theory include undecidable propositions). However, MacIntyre's critique concerns not the fact that there is little correspondence between the one process and the other, but rather concerns the *quality* of generalization in different fields of inquiry and the confidence that can be placed in each. His argument is that there are systems and conventions for accepting or rejecting generalizations in the natural sciences that simply have no parallel in the social sciences, and nor could they have, given the circumstances he outlines. Certainly, the thinking processes of natural scientists, social scientists and those in the humanities may, in reality, not be so very different, as Rorty (1982), Latour and Woolgar (1979), Lynch (1985) and many others have suggested, but there are clear differences in the quality of the generalizations that can be drawn in each arena.

For the special generalization of social science to be worth something, it must involve more than our everyday generalizations and tacit heuristic exercises, for such patternings and such exercises are what human beings do all the time *par excellence*. As Schatzman (1991: 304) notes, we are all the time using 'common interpretive acts' to help us order and comprehend the world. We see links, discover patterns, make generalizations, create explanatory propositions – weak, vernacular or protoscientific theory, if you like – all the time, emerging out of our experience – and it is all involved in the interpretation of a 'case'. The problem for those who are foregrounding generalization in the validation of social science method comes in distinguishing the significance of these explanatory propositions from the putatively *special* generalizations of the social sciences.

If this analysis is correct, neither everyday nor special generalization offers any privilege over the other. The conclusion is that both offer a heuristic or frame of analysis: a way of saying, 'Here is a way of looking at it'. All generalization involves a kind of 'bounded rationality' (Simon, 1983), in that in circumstances of imperfect knowledge people use rules of thumb, heuristics, based on the best available information. While these rest in generalization, they do not pretend to offer *special* prospective or retrospective generalization or the development of theory, with all that this implies, but rather offer a simple process of conjectures and refutations, some of which will prove helpful, some not.

This process of using available information, of course, happens in natural science. Medawar noted – in discussing what scientists say they do versus what they actually do – that the special methods and procedures that are supposed to be associated with scientists' work represent merely 'the postures we choose to be seen in when the curtain goes up and the public sees us' (Medawar, 1982: 88), a point empirically borne out by Latour and Woolgar (1979), Lynch (1985) and others. In other words, the folk model of science is not an accurate representation of what scientists actually do. In fact, natural scientists often do something quite 'un-experiment-like', and more 'case study-like'. As Flyvbjerg (2006) points out, cases and experience were critical to the development of the work of Einstein, Bohr and Darwin. The assertion is supported by Einstein himself, who says that the essence of 'scientific method', '... is in the seeking in whatever manner is suitable, a simplified and lucid image of the world ... There is no logical path, but only intuition' (Holton, 1995: 168). It is worth noting that Einstein's *annus mirabilis* papers (including special relativity and mass-energy equivalence) were produced with little more than 'thought experiments' and a pencil, while Darwin's theory of evolution could be said to have been based upon a series of case studies bonded by what Pólya (2004 [1945]: 172) calls 'brains and good luck'. It involved a process of intuition attributed by Simon (1983) to tacit incremental chunking. Pólya's 'brains' in the intuition comes from curiosity, questioning and surprise, and these phenomena occur when something is found that is not consistent with previous expectations and beliefs – those circumstances occurring in Darwin's case in his discovery, for example, of unusual distributions of species in the Galapagos, followed by his surprise, curiosity, questioning and systematic story-building.

Where the natural scientist's process differs is in what Gilbert Ryle called the valid issue of '*inference tickets*'. Ryle notes that natural scientists have clear methods for establishing these causal links: 'Bacteriologists do discover causal connexions between bacteria and diseases ... and so provide themselves with inference tickets which enable them to infer from diseases to bacteria' (1990: 117). But Ryle's point is that these inference tickets – offering substantial warrant for imputations about causality and its direction – depend for their validity on the quality of the fact-finding and reasoning connected with them. Any *potential* 'causal connections' that may happen to be noticed are in themselves insubstantial; the 'inference ticket', the conclusion about cause, has to be painstakingly enabled by the additional work of a research community which tests alternative hypotheses, replicates, and attempts to falsify. Only after these processes are complete do the grand ambitions of induction in natural science begin to seem realizable.

The problem, says Ryle, is that functional differences between arguments and narratives are often elided in our everyday discourse. And here is the problem for the special generalization of social science. Its generalizations can offer no inference tickets – they enable no prediction or explanation, or at least no better prediction or explanation than any of us would make on the basis of our many years of experience of being human.

Theory and generalizable knowledge

… they hasted to their theories and dogmaticals, and were imperious and scornful toward particulars … [and if they were in error] … they charged the deceit upon the senses, which in my judgment, notwithstanding all their cavillations, are very sufficient to certify and report truth, though not always immediately … But they ought to have charged the deceit upon the weakness of the intellectual powers, and upon the manner of collecting and concluding upon the reports of the senses. (Francis Bacon, 1999 [1605]: 93–4)

Given the difficulties in establishing any kind of special generalization from the endeavours of social science there exists commonly a recourse to *theory*, almost as a proxy for generalization. Indeed, 'theory' has become synonymic with 'generalization' in much social scientific discourse, even though there are clear distinctions to be made about the use of the word ('theory') in different places, distinctions that perhaps enable a circumvention of the arguments that have been made about the legitimacy of generalization in social scientific endeavour. Mouzelis (1995: 2) notes that one of the commonest uses of 'theory' in social science is to denote a proposition – a generalization – which can be proved or disproved by empirical investigation. Used in this way it is a means of using the putative method of natural science, of theorizing following induction, while avoiding 'unfashionable functionalist vocabulary' (ibid: 7). Mouzelis proceeds to suggest that if social scientists use 'theory' in this way they retain the 'fundamental logic [of functionalism] – with the result that crypto-functionalist elements and related distinctions are clandestinely reintroduced into their writings'.

Mouzelis is speaking principally from the perspective of sociology, but the phenomenon he identifies occurs across the social sciences. A good example of the reasoning here, a mini case study, occurs in the writing of the doyen of experimental method in the social sciences, Donald Campbell (though there is no 'crypto' element in Campbell's advocacy of natural scientific method). Campbell, in his transition from pioneer *extraordinaire* in the methodology of the experiment to research methodologist per se, shifted his position during this transition on his understanding of case study. He moved from a position that case studies '… have such a total absence of control as to be of almost no scientific value' (Campbell and Stanley, 1966: 6–7), to one, some years later, in which (in talking about comparative social science) it is '… the only route to knowledge' (Campbell, 1988: 377). He proceeds:

While it is probable that many case studies professing or implying interpretation or explanation, or relating the case to theory, are guilty of these faults, it now seems to me clear that not all are, or need be, and that I have overlooked a major source of discipline ... In a case study done by an alert social scientist who has thorough local acquaintance, the *theory* he uses to explain the focal difference also generates predictions or expectations on dozens of other aspects of the culture, and he does not retain the *theory* unless most of these are also confirmed. ... The process is a kind of pattern matching in which there are many aspects of the pattern demanded by the *theory* that are available for matching with his observations of the local setting. (Campbell, 1988: 380, emphases added)

In Campbell's conversion to the value of case study here, it will be noted that there is an important ingredient in this yielding to its merit. In his ultimate acceptance he is recognizing the value of case study but is doing this only in the context of the establishment of theory. Theory becomes the vehicle by which case study's validity is tested. Theory, as he speaks of it here, means a broad generalization or a previously recognized pattern – one that will 'generate predictions ... on other aspects of the culture' – and this is the template to which the observations made in the case study will have to conform. It then appears that there is the possibility of the theory being dispensed with in a process of Popperian falsification in the face of contradictory observations. The process, then – drawn on widely in validating case study's offer, see Vaughan (1992), Walton (1992) and Eisenhart (2009) – is essentially the same as that which is supposed to occur in natural science, with individual observations confirming or rejecting established theory. The important problem remaining, though, is that it is not clear what processes of judgement would determine whether it should be the case study or the theory that should be reformulated or replaced in the circumstance of discrepancy.

Notwithstanding this issue (or perhaps not seeing it), this is how Campbell came to accommodate himself to the validity of the case study – by slotting it into what is assumed to be the general methodology of natural science. Theory, with its establishment, its confirmation or its rejection is at the heart of this process. Via some kind of connective ganglia the *case* is connected with the *theory*. Does it conform? Is it all right to say, yes, this is like the rest, and it contributes to our accumulating knowledge base? Does it conform to the folk-view of scientific 'theory' – that of the abstracted essence, providing an external, independent guide which rises above the one-off, the local, the parochial, the partisan?

As we have already noted, there are two issues about the assumption of the inductive clothes of the natural scientist in the treatment of generalization and theory. The first issue is about the extent to which the social scientific model can be congruent with the natural scientific model. The second concerns the extent to which the putatively natural scientific model is the actual process by which natural science progresses.

We can return now to Schön (1987) for his explanation of why his graduate student could speak only in generalities: the reason he gives is as follows:

> I think it is because she had been socialized to an institution where, tacitly and auto-matically, we believe that the only thing that really counts and the only thing that's really of value is *theory*, and the higher and the more abstract and the more general the theory, the higher the status it is. Under such conditions it's very difficult to give more or less concrete examples. (Schön, 1987)

Schön is not the first to notice the status accorded to the general account and its place in the establishment of theory. Wittgenstein (1958, 17–19) talked of the 'craving for generality' and the attendant 'contemptuous attitude toward the particular case'. The craving for generality, says Wittgenstein, has 'not only led to no result', but has made us 'dismiss as irrelevant the concrete cases which alone could have helped to understand' (1958: 19–20); 'Nothing is more suspect than too great generality', he said elsewhere (in Waismann, 1984: 103).

The point being made is that we should restrain a first impulse to make abstract, to generalize, to find principles, to synthesize – then to call all of this 'theory' and to engage in a pretence that reliable prediction is possible on the basis of the 'theory'. The process constrains our capacity to examine and to understand the individual, the idiographic.

Phronesis and exemplary knowledge

Our discussion in this section rests on distinctions being drawn between phronesis and theory on the one hand, and generalizable knowledge and exemplary knowledge on the other. We shall come on to the latter distinction in a moment, but will first look at the distinction between phronesis and theory.

Phronesis, as one of us has noted elsewhere (Thomas, 2007), occurs in practising – not just teaching or lecturing, but any practice. In any practice local considerations will always obtain and these will be based on what Hirsch (1976: 18) calls '... making calculations of probability based on an insider's knowledge'. Or, in Fish's terms by '... extending a practice, employing a set of heuristic questions [always] ... tethered to the contextual setting' (1989: 322–3). Teachers are reflective practitioners, develop-ing and using phronesis. Fish (1989: 317) suggests that the tacit knowledge and rules of thumb used on the basis of phronesis 'vary with the contextual circumstances of an ongoing practice; as those circumstances change, the very meaning of the rule (the instructions it is understood to give) changes too'.

Phronesis thus exists in the person of the researcher and the reader, and it is here that we see the 'transferability' and 'fittingness' spoken about by Lincoln and Guba (1985: 124) in the context of case study coming into play, with the emphasis on the intersubjectivities kindled in these relationships in case study research and reading. In their seminal work, Berger and Luckmann (1979: 20) suggested that 'the foundations of knowledge in everyday life' are constructed out of 'subjective processes (and mean-ings) by which the intersubjective commonsense world is constructed' – meanings that provide 'multiple realities'. They argue that understanding is built out of diverse heuristics and thinking tools occurring across the cultural spectrum, from language to reminiscence, folk tales, proverbs and professional vocabularies.

Such building blocks are drawn on and married together variously as we conduct our everyday and our research lives. The view from here is inevitably different from the view from there. The consequence was summed up by Schutz (1964: 93) some time before Berger and Luckmann when he said: ' ... the knowledge of the man who acts and thinks within the world of his daily life is not homogeneous; it is (1) incoherent, (2) only partially clear, and (3) not at all free from contradictions.' It is all of these things because it is contextually located: it is personal.

Starting with Schutz's notion of social knowledge as inevitably only partially clear permits one to look with less procedural self-consciousness for alternative ways of seeking corrigible interpretation, analysis and action – ways based in phronesis. The hallmark should be in malleability. Social scientific inquirers in the conduct of case studies should be satisfied – no, *pleased* – with what Bacon called 'middle axioms' (see Wormald, 1993; Hirsch, 1976: 18). Middle axioms are the generalizations that can be applied if one understands the context in which they are framed: there should be no surfeit of enthusiasm for their universal applicability. As Bacon put it of middle axioms: '... in every knowledge and science, and in the rules and axioms appertaining to them, a mean must be kept between too many distinctions and too much generality' (cited in Wormald, 1993: 105).

But more is needed than simply a middle way. It is a recognition of a need for provisional, tentative models for interpretation and analysis. These provide for assumptions of variability in the interpretation of exemplary knowledge, variations in what Gadamer (1975: 269) calls the 'horizon of meaning'.

We should make it clear that in 'exemplary knowledge' we are talking about an example *viewed and heard* in the context of another's experience (another's horizon) but *used* in the context of one's own (where the horizon changes): the example is not taken to be representative, typical or standard, nor is it exemplary in the sense of being a model or an exemplar. It is not, in other words, taken to be what Lincoln and Guba (1985) assert of generalization – that is to say that '... generalizations are assertions of *enduring* value that are *context-free*' (1985: 110, original emphasis). Rather, it is taken to be a particular representation given in context and understood in that context. However, it is interpretable only in the context of one's own experience – in the context, in other words, of one's phronesis, rather than one's theory.

Stake (1995: 85) discusses something similar here in his 'naturalistic generalization', which he describes thus: 'Naturalistic generalizations are conclusions arrived at through personal engagement in life's affairs or by vicarious experience so well constructed that the person feels as if it happened to themselves'. He proceeds to note that Hamilton uses the term to refer to 'understandings that are private'. However, it is possible to see more than private meanings in exemplary knowledge. We can see meaning that is malleable and interpretable in the context of experience. The case study thus offers an example from which one's experience, one's phronesis, enables one to gather insight or understand a problem.

Where does this leave us, in practical terms, if we speak about phronesis rather than theory – if theoretical analysis is de-coupled from the case study ground? It leaves us with a view of case study incorporating and using a number of ideas. Rather than seeking the case study's validation through reference to a body of theory or generalized knowledge, case study can offer a series of ways of proceeding based in exemplary knowledge. It offers a validation for making connections between another's experience and one's own, seeing links, having insights. The essence comes in understandability emerging from phronesis – in other words, from the connection to one's own situation due to phronesis. This is all based in what Abbott (1992) calls colligations of occurrences, involving the making of narrative – the development of stories with which one can connect. This is a characteristic, he notes, of all social science, intelligently done, whether it be 'positivist' or interpretivist. In an entertaining analysis, he dissects key sentences in some 'standard positivist articles' (ibid: 54), inspecting them for their subjects and their predicates and noting how those predicates are related to causality. Abbott does this in order to uncover implicit 'case assumptions' operating in these analysts' minds. Unsurprisingly, they are discovered throughout the range of their work. One might almost say that it is endemic, and – rather than being critical about this unacknowledged assumption – one should perhaps note that this is surely the *sine qua non* of good social scientific inquiry. It should, in other words, routinely make these connections, make assumptions about people thinking, having beliefs and motives, making choices – people with histories and interests, with different 'horizons of meaning', people who have agency. Abbott does a service in showing empirically how prevalent such implicit assumptions are in all inquiry and how near to the surface they are.

These assumptions are revealed during inquiry by what Abbott calls 'causal narrativity' (ibid: 57). While he gives few clues as to its anatomy, it is this that is surely at the root of method in case study: it is this that we should be looking for in a case study. For us, and on the basis of the argument set out earlier in this chapter, it is not generality that is at the heart of case study. Nor, in an acknowledgement of the impossibility of special generalization, can any recourse be made to theory, for theory in this context is being used to mean simply 'a generalization' – weak or strong (a distinction made by Cicourel, 1979, in relation to kinds of theory that tie together inductive assumptions). Rather, case study offers understanding presented from another's 'horizon of meaning', but understood from one's own.

Conclusion

The *generalizability criterion* is central in validating the offer of social science. Case study has found difficulty in meeting this criterion and has rested its status epistemologically instead in its contribution to a certain kind of theory. Such theory proffers the generalizability criterion in a different form, retaining a distinction between what we might call *everyday generalization* and *special generalization* but loosening demands for clarity about the quantifiers and modifiers or exceptions to the theory where that putatively special generalization is being discovered.

But critics of social science method have argued that special generalization in social science is an illusory goal: it is not possible in *any kind* of social inquiry. If this argument is valid it frees idiographic inquiry from the expectational skeins that accompany the generalizability criterion. From here, we have proceeded to argue that to seek *generalizable knowledge*, in whatever form – everyday or special – is to miss the point about what may be offered by certain kinds of inquiry, which is *exemplary knowledge*. The articulation and exegesis of that exemplary knowledge rests in the phronesis of the researcher ... and its understanding in the phronesis of the reader.

The distinction between theory and phronesis is important as an unproblematized notion of *theory* increasingly marks what is supposed to be special in the academic's offer (see the notes of the Education panel from the 2008 UK Research Assessment Exercise: HEFCE, 2009). But the argument we have made in this chapter is that the particular contribution of the social scientist depends on theory less than it does on phronesis. Why should one person's analysis of an educational question be any better than an architect's or a zookeeper's, given the lack of distinction we have noted between everyday and special generalization? It emerges neither from theoretical sophistication nor from the vigilance with which that person restricts their reading to research endorsed by the Campbell Collaboration. Rather, it emerges from – for example – having been a teacher and tried various kinds of teaching, having observed in hundreds of classrooms, having read *A Glasgow Gang Observed*, perhaps having been a parent and a school governor, having read papers using multi-level modelling to explain a phenomenon – and others asserting that the first papers are nonsense. This is the phronesis of the academic researcher's offer. One person's is different from another's, and always will be.

It is this phronesis that enables the construction of the good case study, its critical reading and its use. But the study must be framed not in the diluted constructs of generalizing natural science but rather in questioning and surprise, heuristic, particularity, analogy, consonance or dissonance with one's own situation.

FOUR

Induction and the case study

The validity of case study as a respectable form of social science inquiry rests in its ability, like other forms of inquiry, to use a form of induction in developing theory. In this chapter we extend the argument of the last chapter to argue that social science inquiry does not in fact use induction and does not develop theory. Rather, it uses abduction and develops phronesis.

Distinctions between abduction and induction, and between phronesis and theory are often elided in methodological discussion about case study. Making these distinctions clear offers a pathway for the better conduct of case study and for a less apologetic stance in its use. Owing its legitimacy to the experiential knowledge of phronesis rather than the generalizing power of induction and theory in explanation and prediction, case study can more unself-consciously look to the anatomy of narrative for the justification of its processes and its conclusions. A look at this anatomy reveals a number of ways in which the valency of case study may be constructed.

***

In his novel *The Unbearable Lightness of Being*, Milan Kundera makes this point:

> *Einmal ist keinmal.* What happens but once might as well not have happened at all. The history of the Czechs will not be repeated, nor will the history of Europe. The history of the Czechs and of Europe is a pair of sketches from the pen of mankind's fateful inexperience. History is as light as individual human life, unbearably light, light as a feather, as dust swirling into the air, as whatever will no longer exist tomorrow. (Kundera, 1984)

Kundera's account of the limitations of interpreting from 'what happens once' is of course in many senses valid – in fact, they are at the root of the poor-relation status of the case study as a way of conducting research. The history of the Czechs will not be repeated insofar as the particulars are concerned. This is not to say, though, that patterns and connections do not exist between the history of the Czechs and that of others. The specific circumstances about which Kundera wrote, namely, the conditions of a repressed state, have been repeated and were characteristic of a clutch of Eastern European states.

But the large consequences of repression and upheaval are predictable not *exclusively* by the social scientist: they are evident to anyone with eyes (or at least with an eye to history). It is the specifics in which Kundera – and the social scientist – are interested. And these specifics are understandable only in terms of their particulars – those provided by the case and understood in terms of the experience of the observer. It is mutual if idiosyncratic understanding that marks out the offer of case study for the social scientist, and this must not be lost in an unrealizable search for generalization.

***

Despite case study's popularity as a method it persists with something of an aura of methodological second-best about it – for reasons resting in the *Einmal ist keinmal* on which Kundera draws and which we reviewed in Chapter 3. The concern is that one is focusing on the single case. The focus on the singular is captured well in Stake's (2005) typology of case study in three essential forms: intrinsic, instrumental and multiple. As Stake puts it, 'Case study is not a methodological choice but a choice of what is to be studied' (2005: 443) and whether we study the case for its intrinsic interest (that is to say, his 'intrinsic case study') or to provide insight into an issue (his 'instrumental case study'), generalization is not possible.

The point we tried to make in Chapter 3 is that it is the inability of case study to offer generalizable findings that is at the core of the argument against this form of research as an instrument of serious inquiry. We argue now that the reason for case study's poor-relation status rests in the attempt of most social science to offer *induction* from generalization. But it is only if one takes as valid the aim of induction that case study can be taken to be a 'poor relation', since it is *conspicuously* deficient in its potential for generalization. Its weaknesses, in other words, are not disguised. Other design frames in social science seek ways of calibrating and enabling generalization, but these attempts at generalization rest on something of a sleight of hand in the presentation of what induction is, what generalization can be, and what theory is. If, as we have already argued, little significant generalization is possible in the human sciences, arguments about case study's deficiencies in this department lose force.

Our point is that when thinking about inference, generalization in social inquiry is constrained to remain at the level of what Peirce (see Houser et al., 1992) called 'abduction' rather than induction. We argue that the goal of social scientific endeavour, particularly in the study of cases, should be exemplary knowledge unself-consciously based on abduction gained and offered through phronesis rather than through theory.

If our argument has validity then there are forms of interpretation that can come from case study that owe their legitimacy and power to the exemplary knowledge of case study, rather than to its generalizability. The seeking of generalizability can inhibit or even extinguish the curiosity and interpretation that can come from phronesis. At the end of the chapter we outline some of the means of interpretation – or causal narrativity as Abbott (1992) has called it – that can guide case study's construction and use.

Generalization, induction and abduction

Expectations surrounding generalization (reviewed in Chapter 3) are constrained by the sheer contingency of social life and human agency. The problem here is in expectations of watertight (or almost watertight) induction following generalization. Perhaps, following Peirce (see Houser et al., 1992), our expectations should be more moderated concerning the generalizations that can emerge from social study. A number of commentators have queried the reliance on a naïve model of scientific induction (see for example, Haig, 1995), and others such as Miller and Fredericks (1999), point to the lack of 'specialness' of inductive reasoning. The thrust of their argument is that common, everyday induction is better described as 'inference to the best explanation', or Peirce's 'abduction'. This kind of limited generalization is only at what Peirce (1992 [1878]) calls the second grade of clarity in the pragmatic account. It does not achieve, while still at this level (using abduction) the third and final grade in the pragmatic account wherein a full range of additional conditional propositions might follow. This third grade aligns with induction. It is in the acknowledgement of the distinction between abduction and induction that Peirce offers guidance on the pragmatic limits of inquiry – an acknowledgement that enables a focus-setting about the place, nature and limits of our inquiries.

Hammersley (2005: 5) suggests that '… what is good evidence for abduction is different from what is good evidence for induction' proceeding to describe abduction as '… the development of an explanatory or theoretical idea, this often resulting from close examination of particular cases.' (See also Hammersley, 2007.) It could, perhaps simplistically, be thought of as 'conclusions drawn from everyday generalization', whereas induction concerns conclusions drawn from a special kind of generalization, aligning with Ryle's 'inference tickets' and Peirce's 'third grade' of pragmatism – a kind, if MacIntyre is right, which is impossible in the social sciences.

It seems to us that any argument about the weakness of case study that rests on its lack of generalizability fails to recognize the limits of induction in social science generally, and fails simultaneously to acknowledge the significance of abduction. It fails, in other words, to recognize the offer that can be made in local circumstances by particular kinds of looser generalization, whatever one calls these. We have chosen to use Peirce's term 'abduction' for these to foreground the contra-distinctions to be made with *in*duction in discussing the putative weaknesses of case study, but they have been framed in many other ways, from Bacon's 'middle axioms', to Piaget's 'schema' to Hirsch's 'local hermeneutics'. Indeed, Hirsch (1976) calls for a bringing together of ideas summarized in what he calls 'corrigible schemata':

> It is very remarkable how widespread is the pattern I have been discussing ... no doubt an hypothesis is not just the same as Husserl's 'intentional object', which in turn is not exactly the same as Piaget's 'schema', Dilthey's 'whole', or Heidegger's 'pre-understanding'. Yet important features of all these proposals are quite identical in their character and function, and also in their connection with what we call meaning. (Hirsch, 1976: 35)

Other ideas can be added: the 'common interpretive act' (Schatzman, 1991); 'bounded rationality' (Simon, 1983); Bourdieu's 'thinking tool' (in Wacquant, 1989: 50); or Althusser's Generalities II (Althusser, 1979: 183–90). All describe much the same kind of process: a fluid understanding that explicitly or tacitly recognizes the complexity and frailty of the generalizations we can make about human interrelationships. Even in discussing the scope and limits of computational psychology, Fodor (2001: 28) discusses the linkages between the '"global" or "abductive" or "holistic" or "inferences to the best explanation"', noting that 'a mental representation is *not* determined by its individuating properties' (ibid, original emphasis).

They describe our processes of garnering and organizing information to analyze and deal with our social worlds. Abduction connects all of these, providing heuristics – ways of analyzing complexity that may not provide watertight guarantees of success in providing for explanation or predication, but are unpretentious in their assumptions of fallibility and provisionality.

All of these forms of generalizing to regularity – these kinds of abduction – seem the appropriate inferential form for case study.

Phronesis not theory

In the traditional account of the process of science that we have described, the end point of the inductive process results in theory. Seen in the way that Peirce (1992 [1878]) presents it, abduction generates ideas, tentative 'theories', which serve as hypothetical explanatory concepts. This abduction is then followed by deduction, which is followed in turn by systematic data collection in pursuit of verification of the initial explanatory concepts. This last is induction, via which the speculative theory is or is not verified.

The assumption that this is the course things invariably take seems to lead always into the dead end identified by MacIntyre. In other words, the assumption of theoretical validation from inductive inference necessarily implies a firmness to the structure and reliability of theory which is unachievable in the inquiries of social science. Because of both the contingency of social life and the necessary limitations on the kind and quantity of confirmatory evidence that can be disclosed, theory, in any kind of technical sense, is unattainable. There is an elision of expectation here in the discussion of theory. As one of us have noted elsewhere (Thomas and James, 2006; Thomas, 2007), a reading of interpretative inquiry scholarship from Glaser and Strauss (1967: 1) onwards (see Mouzelis, 1995) reveals an insistent theme in expectations of theoretical explanation and prediction from induction.

Of course, something is attainable, but the question is, 'Is it theory?' It can be theory only in the sense that everything is theory. Fish (1989) suggests that much discourse about theory in the academy generally is not really about theory at all, but rather about 'theory-talk' – that is, 'any form of talk that has acquired cachet and prestige' (1989: 14–15). He proceeds:

> Am I following or enacting a theory when I stop for a red light, or use my American Express card, or rise to speak at a conference? Are you now furiously theorizing as you sit reading what I have to say? And if you are persuaded by me to alter your understanding of what is and is not a theory, is your new definition of theory a new theory of theory? Clearly it is possible to answer yes to all these questions, but just as clearly that answer will render the notion 'theory' and the issue of its consequences trivial by making 'theory' the name for ordinary, contingent, unpredictable, everyday behavior. (Fish, 1989: 327)

In other words, theory has come to mean almost anything – any generalization, any thought, any structured reflection (or indeed unstructured reflection) may be called theory. But it is unhelpful in our deliberations on inquiry for looseness to exist about the terms we use – in this case, 'theory' – particularly when separating abduction from induction and looking to the end point of induction. The process of induction is supposed to lead us to theory of a particular character – theory that summarizes and generalizes in such a way that we are able to use it to explain and predict. It confuses our deliberations on inquiry to call *any* kind of summative or generalizing process 'theory'. When theory has been used as part of the reasoning used to validate case study (see, for example, Vaughan, 1992; Walton, 1992; Eisenhart, 2009) it has indeed been as part of this summative, inductive, or quasi-inductive process.

It is worth returning to MacIntyre's (1985) analysis here, since it speaks to the central problem with generalization and theory in the social sciences. He notes that there are four reasons for the failure of theory (that is to say, theory as part of a quasi-inductive process), all resting in 'systematic unpredictability' in the social world. First, there is nature of radical conceptual innovation: it is impossible to predict because a necessary part of prediction must involve the incorporation of the prediction itself. Second, agents are unable to predict their own behaviour, let alone that of others. This introduces radical contingency into any event. Third, the illusoriness of the game-theoretic character of social life; in short, 'Not one game is being played, but several' with several sets of rules and with no determinate, enumerable set of factors, the totality of which comprise the situation. Fourth, there is pure contingency – the things of everyday life that cannot be factored into any situation.

Because of these, he suggests, unpredictability will always win over predictability as far as the matters of social science are concerned. It is only the trivial things that are predictable, and we don't need any kind of sophisticated methodology to tell us about these. What characterizes the subjects of social science is 'pervasive unpredictability'. This renders all projection in social life 'permanently vulnerable and fragile' (MacIntyre, 1985: 103).

If this critique has any legitimacy, a distinction, in response, can be made between theory and phronesis, as we noted in Chapter 3. The Aristotelian notion of phronesis is about practical knowledge, craft knowledge, with a twist of judgement squeezed in to the mix. As it has been used more recently, particularly in the discussion of the applied social sciences (see, for example, Back, 2002) it has come to have more of a sense of 'tacit knowledge' (Polanyi, 1958) about it. Sometimes, confusingly, it is called 'practical theory'. It still involves, Grundy (1987) suggests, 'discernment', or the ability to weigh up, to judge, to assess implicitly. It is judgement made on the basis of experience and without recourse to the external guide that theory putatively provides. It is in practice that phronesis is developed and in practice that it comes into play. Back proceeds to provide a contrast between phronesis and theory, explaining that in Aristotelian terms 'theory' exists as a way of establishing absolute laws that can be laid out in an organized framework which can explain. It must be able to withstand tests as to its validity, and it needs to be consistent. By contrast, in the practical (or tacit) knowledge of phronesis there are none of these expectations as to consistency; phronesis is about understanding and behaviour in particular situations.

Fish's explication of practical learning analyzes the contrast well (1989: 317) for he explains how practical learning varies with the context of a practice. As circumstances change, so '... the very meaning of the rule (the instructions it is understood to give) changes too'. In other words, the phronesis that we acquire and accumulate is always malleable and corrigible. So there is, in talking about phronesis, a recognition of the provisional, the tentative in interpretation and analysis; there are presumptions of variability in the interpretation of exemplary knowledge, variations in what Gadamer (1975: 269) calls the 'horizon of meaning'. As Pascal (2005 [1658]: 19) put it in his *Pensées*: 'The truth on this side of the Pyrenees, error on the other'.

There is in other words a need to move away from the expectations of *generalizable* knowledge that go alongside inductive process. Correspondingly, there is a need to move toward the '*exemplary* knowledge' of abduction and phronesis. With the discussion of 'exemplary knowledge' we are talking about an example viewed and heard in the context of another's experience – another's horizon, in Gadamer's terms – but *used* in the context of one's own, where the horizon changes: the example is not taken to be representative or typical, nor is it exemplary in the sense of being a model to follow. Rather, it is taken to be a particular representation given in context and understood in that context. However, it is interpretable only in the context of one's own experience – in the context, in other words, of one's phronesis, rather than theory.

In exemplary knowledge are meanings that are malleable and interpretable in the context of varieties of experience. The case study thus offers an example from which one's experience, one's phronesis, enables one to gather insight or understand a problem.

If case study is concerned with phronesis rather than theory – if it is de-coupled from the inductive frame of theoretical analysis – what are the consequences? We are left with a view of case study's validation coming no longer through reference to a body of theory or generalized knowledge; its validation comes through the connections and insights it offers between another's experience and one's own. The essence comes in understandability emerging from phronesis – in other words, from the connection to one's own situation.

Doing and interpreting case study: the anatomy of narrative

What then should be at the heart of case study, focusing especially on the causal narrativity of Abbott? In the following, and borrowing especially from Bruner (1991), we suggest some key ingredients to a phronesis-based case study. It is an anatomy, if you like, of case narrativity, of story-making, using abduction (rather than expecting induction) and relying on phronesis (rather than expecting the development of theory).

Questioning and surprise; intelligent noticing and serendipity

'Our brightest blazes of gladness are commonly kindled by unexpected sparks' said Samuel Johnson (1963 [1759]). When inventors and creative thinkers give us an insight into the ways that they think, it is clear that the role of generalization, if it is at all significant, is subservient to metaphor, inspiration, imagination and even dream. Storr (1997: 176) provides many examples of this kind of intuition in which a solution suddenly appears. He quotes from the mathematician Gauss: 'Like a sudden flash of lightning, the riddle happened to be solved. I myself cannot say what was the conducting thread which connected what I previously knew with what made my success possible'. The same happens in social practice and inquiry, and the case study seems the ideal vehicle for this kind of insight to occur, as long as it is enabled by a spirit of inquisitiveness and not extinguished in a search for generality. Questioning is the starting point; serendipity, noticing and insight provide an elevation; and interpretation based on phronesis is the key.

Heuristic and incremental chunking

Heuristic is from the Greek *heuriskein*, meaning to discover. Archimedes's sojourn in the bath could be seen as presenting him with a kind of discovery in case study, or, in Einstein's terms, a 'thought experiment' (which is, of course, nothing like a true experiment, and more like a dynamic thought-example). And he jumped out of the bath shouting 'Eureka!', meaning 'I've found it'. The 'I've found it!' of Eureka is related to today's meaning of heuristics in an explanatory device – albeit one that is assumed to be corrigible and 'for the time being'. We are not being facetious, we hope, in pointing out that Archimedes did not leap from his bath, shouting 'I have a theory!' His 'Eureka!' was about explanation, pure and simple, arising from observation and insight arising from abduction. It is similar (though perhaps unflatteringly) to Köhler's apes' 'Ah Ha!' – see Köhler (1925). This 'Ah Ha' of intuition, if dissected, is similar to Simon's (1983) tacit processes of incremental chunking. It is the putting together of related information to make a story. Bruner also calls this story-making *hermeneutic composability*: how does a series of events merge into a story? How are the elements woven together, if at all? What appears to depend on what? What contradicts? Where are the paradoxes?

Narrative diachronicity

Change occurs over time. The case inquirer is aware of this, is cognizant of change with time, notices change as it happens and seeks its correlates and its sequelae. It is a question of finding the 'sequence of steps' as Becker puts it (1992: 209) and conjecturing about what is related to what. Becker calls the resulting analysis a 'tree diagram', wherein each step is understood as preceding in time the one that follows. As he puts it elsewhere:

> Assume that whatever you want to study has, not causes, but a history, a story, a narrative, a 'first this happened, then that happened, and then the other happened, and it ended up like this.' On this view we understand the occurrence of events by learning the steps in the process by which they came to happen, rather than by learning the conditions that made their existence necessary. (Becker, 1998: 60–1)

Particularity

Let us repeat part of our quotation from novelist Iris Murdoch's (2002) *Under the Net*: 'All theorising is flight. We must be ruled by the situation itself and this is unutterably particular.' There is, in other words, uniqueness to the particular situation, and one should seek to understand this without what Oakeshott (1967: 2) calls the 'irritable search for order'. One should not judge this situation and its significance by reference to others. One should understand it, returning to the quotation from Kundera at the beginning of this chapter, by reference to the particular.

The focus on the particular requires a special effort of will for the professional or student researcher, given the predilection to establish, develop and refer to theory amongst social scientists. Bourdieu (1992: 233–4) puts it well in suggesting that analysis should not be through '… the extraneous and artificial application of formal and empty constructions', but rather through thinking about the particular case as a 'particular instance of the possible'.

Intentional state entailment

We should observe, Bruner (1991) notes, not just what people do, but more importantly what they think and feel. It is their beliefs, desires and values that are important. There is nothing different here from the thick description of the ethnographer. It should be the unself-conscious hallmark of the case studier, not a means-to-an-end in the pursuit of what is assumed to really matter: theoretical development.

Canonicity, breach and counterfactuality

Case studies, as narratives, have a function in enabling a recognition and an understanding of where the case differs from what is normal or expected. How and why is this so? What does the phronesis of the inquirer tell us about this difference? Feyerabend (1993) suggests that we may use 'counterrules': hypotheses that contradict well-established thinking of one kind or another). Kuhn (1970: 52) suggested something similar in a need for the 'awareness of anomaly'.

Canonicity and breach can be made more structured by the deliberate introduction of an imaginary breach to the established position or the understanding. This is taken up in various fields in the use of counterfactuals (see Kahneman and Tversky, 1973; Byrne, 2005; Mandel et al., 2005), that is to say in the imagination of a state of affairs which would exist had a particular event (usually a key one) not occurred – in other words, 'What if …?' questions. The idea has been foregrounded by historians (e.g. Ferguson, 1999) and although it is mentioned by Ragin (2007: 63) it has not been widely used as part of case study method in the social sciences.

Context sensitivity and negotiability

Perhaps in the same way that Barthes (1974) talks about 'writerly' texts (as distinct from 'readerly' texts), in which the meaning is created by the reader, so the assumption should be that the interpretation of the case is embedded in the inquirer's (and the reader's) own experiences. Interpretation is personal – again, located in the phronesis of the inquirer – and is not licensed via reference to an archive of theory. It is the context sensitivity that enables readers to make sense of the narrative of the case, and then agree or disagree with the researcher.

Analogy

One case will be compared with another and compared with our own experience. We make sense of the unfamiliar by reference to the familiar, by way of drawing personal analogy. Tavor Bannet (1997: 655) makes an interesting analysis of Wittgenstein's and Derrida's discussions of what happens during analogy. For Wittgenstein, she says, analogy is not just the juxtaposition of objects for comparison. It is a ' ... method of reasoning from the known to the unknown, and from the visible to the speculative' by carrying familiar terms and images across into unfamiliar territory. In a similar vein, she notes, Derrida describes analogy as a form of translation: '... a way of transporting something from place to place, from old to new, from original to copy, and from one (con)text to another' (ibid). It is the process of bringing together, juxtaposing, seeing similarities across contexts, that conspicuously happens during reading of case study.

Conclusion

Much of the discussion in this chapter has been about trying to resolve what Lincoln and Guba (1985) call the 'nomothetic-ideographic dilemma'. Bourdieu (in Wacquant, 1989: 36) sees this more as a 'false antinomy' than a dilemma: the opposition between the universal and the unique, between nomothetic analysis and ideographic description, is a false opposition, he suggests. And the way out of this contrived discord is to 'allow' a different form of reasoning, incorporating the relational and the analogical. By pointing to the legitimacy of the abductive and a shift in emphasis from the theoretical to the phronetic we have tried here to argue for legitimacy in the epistemological stance of the case inquirer. There should be less self-consciousness and less apology about the use of case study. There is no need to adopt and subsume the credentials of inductivist thinking when using case inquiry: it can stand on its own as a method based in the phronesis both of the inquirer and the reader.

FIVE

A typology for case study

In this chapter, we go into detail on the typology introduced in Chapter 1. We disaggregate the various layers of classificatory principle for case studies which are discussed in the literature. We first distinguish two parts of the case study: (i) the *subject* of the study, which is the case itself; and (ii) the *object*, which is the analytical frame or theory through which the subject is viewed and which the subject explicates. Beyond this distinction the case study is presented as classifiable by its purposes and the approaches adopted – principally with a distinction drawn between theory-centred and illustrative study. Beyond this, there are distinctions to be drawn among various operational structures that concern comparative versus non-comparative versions of the form and the ways that the study may employ time.

The need for a typology

Case study research is one of the principal means by which inquiry is conducted in the social sciences. Reviewing work in economics and political science (Acemoglu et al., 2003; Rodrik, 2003; Bates et al., 1998), Gerring (2004: 341) concludes that the use of case study is 'solidly ensconced and, perhaps, even thriving.' Bennett et al. (2003) showed that in 14 journals focusing on two areas of research in social science, the proportion of articles in which a case study was employed remained broadly stable at around 20 per cent over the period 1975–2000.

Despite the popularity of the case study design frame, there is little in the way of organizational structure to guide the intending case inquirer. Gerring continues his review with the telling comment with which we began this book: 'Practitioners continue to ply their trade but have difficulty articulating what it is that they are doing, methodologically speaking. The case study survives in a curious methodological limbo' (2004: 341). de Vaus (2001: 219) agrees, in discussing the way that the case study is explained: 'Most research methods texts either ignore case studies or confuse them with other types of social research.'

If 'methodological limbo' exists it is not for lack of methodological discussion. Indeed, this has been extensive over the last 50 years across the social sciences – see, for example, Simons (2009), Yin (2009), Flyvbjerg (2006), Mitchell (2006), George and Bennett (2005), Stake (2005), Hammersley and Gomm (2000), Bassey (1999), Ragin and Becker (1992), Merriam (1988), Eckstein (1975) and Lijphart (1971). The problem is perhaps that methodological discussion of case study has tended to focus on its epistemological status, its generalizing 'power', or on various aspects of study construction. Less conspicuous, though, has been any synthesis of the discussion which might offer classificatory schemata for intending researchers: there have been only limited attempts to offer intending inquirers a Gestalt, mapping out the terrain and potential routes to travel. By way of response to this state of affairs, we overview here some of the ways in which case study is discussed and defined in order to propose a framing structure and typology for case study. In doing this we attempt to disentangle the threads and layers of classificatory principle that have become interwoven in dialogue about the place and use of the case study.

Back to definitions

In Chapter 1, in discussing what a case study is, we introduced the idea of the difference between the subject and the object of a case study. We won't repeat that discussion here, but it is important to stress the significance of the separateness of the subject and the object in case study since the distinction between the one and the other is characteristic of all social inquiry, yet relatively neglected in discussion of the case study. It is defined variously in different kinds of research. In his classic work on sociological theory, Wallace (1969: 3) pinpointed the significance of the distinction between (i) the thing to be explained and (ii) the explanation in a piece of research, by calling the thing to be explained the *explanandum* and the thing doing the explaining the *explanans*. Some time earlier, Hempel and Oppenheim (1948) had drawn attention to the need for such a differentiation to account for the ability of science to answer 'why' rather than simply 'what' questions. In social science – where we also want to answer 'why' rather than 'what' questions – one of the more straightforward means of making this distinction is by differentiation between dependent and independent variables, yet this of course is not the only way of doing it, and case inquirers need to be aware of this.

Case inquirers need to be aware of it because Wallace went further, aligning the explanandum with the dependent variable, and the explanans with the independent variable, and Eckstein (1975) refers to the analytical frame *in a case study* as a single measure on *a variable*. But one surely needs to be guarded in the use of terms associated with variable-led research when thinking about idiographic research. The extension of explanandum and explanans to putative variables by Wallace (and many after him) is, perhaps, metaphorical. But if this is so – if it is indeed a metaphor – it is a dangerous one if extended to all kinds of research, including the idiographic. In fact, here it becomes more like catachresis than metaphor: let us take the example again of the Second World War (subject) as a case study of a 'just war' (object). Here, the notion of justness is the explanandum (the thing to be explained), and the thing doing the explaining – the explanans – is WWII. This is a quite valid use of the explanandum/explanans distinction as promoted by Hempel and Oppenheim and Wallace. But the idea that the explanans can be seen as an independent variable so grossly violates expectations of an independent variable (for example, singular rather than complex; manipulable experimentally) that it ceases to be tenable.

Likewise, use of the similar term 'unit' is confusing, being adopted by Wieviorka (1992) to refer to the case (the subject), while VanWynsberghe and Khan (2007: 87), for example, use it to mean the object. (They say: 'the interplay between the unit of analysis and *the case* is a constitutive element of case study research' [emphasis added].) These confusions have arisen partly because of the neopositivist discourse surrounding so much methodological discussion concerning case study, of which the 'variable-led' discussion of explanans and explanandum is an example. As another example, look at Lijphart's (1971: 684) distinction between experimental, statistical and comparative method in social science, in which he asserts that, in areas such as political history, comparative method has to be 'resorted to' because of the small number of potential cases and the invalidity of 'credible controls'. Lijphart's analysis is discussed in more detail later.

The ostensible looseness of the case study as a form of inquiry and the conspicuous primacy given to the case (the subject) is perhaps a reason for inexperienced social inquirers, especially students, to neglect to establish any kind of *object* (literally and technically) for their inquiries. Identifying only a *subject*, they fail to seek to explain anything, providing instead, therefore, a simple description in place of a piece of research. For the study to constitute research, there has to be something to be explained (an object) and something potentially to offer explanation (the analysis of the circumstances of a subject).

In brief, as a conclusion to this discussion, we are suggesting that a case study must comprise two elements:

1. a 'practical, historical unity', which we shall call the *subject* of the case study; and
2. an analytical or theoretical frame, which we shall call the *object* of the study.

Taking account of this, we repeat here the definition of case study that we gave in Chapter 1 and which we shall adopt for the typology:

> Case studies are analyses of persons, events, decisions, periods, projects, policies, institutions or other systems which are studied holistically by one or more methods. The case that is the subject of the inquiry will be an instance of a class of phenomena that provides an analytical frame – an object – within which the study is conducted and which the case illuminates and explicates.

We give below an explication of some of the elements and dimensions just discussed, noting points about the kinds of selection and decision likely to be necessary during the case study. This is done to provide a rationale for the typology ultimately summarized in Figure 5.1.

The subject and object

Subject

In making a central distinction between subject and object of study, the definition at which we have arrived leads us first into questions about how the subject is identified – whether that subject is a Glasgow gang (Patrick, 1973), the Head Start education programme (Zigler and Muenchow, 1992), or an international coffee organization (Bates, 1998). The subject is in no sense a sample, representative of a wider population. Rather, the *subject* will be selected because it is an interesting or unusual or revealing example through which the lineaments of the *object* can be refracted. In this, its scope is not restricted: as White (1992) points out, the subject may be as broad as Lenin's analysis of peasant social formations, or as narrow as one of Goffman's smiles. There are three potential routes for selection of the subject.

The first route in its selection may be followed because of the researcher's familiarity with it – a *local knowledge case* – and this will be relevant particularly for the practitioner or student researcher. In one's own place of work, one's placement, or even one's home, there will be intimate knowledge and ample opportunity for informed, in-depth analysis; ample opportunity for identification and discussion, in the words of Bates et al. (1998: 13–14), of '... the actors, the decision points they faced, the choices they made, the paths taken and shunned, and the manner in which their choices generated events and outcomes.' The local knowledge case is eminently amenable to the 'soak and poke' of Fenno (1986, 1990) since the inquirer is already soaked, and in a good position, one hopes, to poke.

Second, the subject may come into focus because of the inherent interest of the case – it may be a *key case* of a phenomenon or, third, may illuminate the object by virtue of its difference, its *outlier* status. The latter is what Lijphart (1971: 692) refers to as the *deviant* case. The essence in both types is in gaining what we call elsewhere in this book 'exemplary knowledge:' the 'key-ness' or 'outlier-ness' of the case is manifested in its capacity to exemplify the analytical object of the inquiry. This ability to exemplify draws its legitimacy from the phronesis of the case inquirer (together with that of the reader of the case inquiry) and we have argued that the exemplary knowledge thus drawn is distinct from the generalizable knowledge associated with induction. While opinions on the significance of generalization in case study differ (compare Gomm et al., 2000; de Vaus, 2001; Flyvbjerg, 2006; and Yin, 2009) – with discussion of varieties of generalization spanning naturalistic generalization (Stake, 1995) to holographic generalization (Lincoln and Guba, 1985) to fuzzy generalization (Bassey, 2001) – we have argued that the validity of the case study cannot derive from its representativeness since it can never legitimately be claimed to form a representative sample from a larger set. The essence of selection must rest in the dynamic of the relation between subject and object. It cannot rest in typicality.

In this choice of the subject, then, we disagree with Yin (2009: 48) when he suggests that a case may be selected because it is *'representative* or *typical'*. Even if we know that a case is following some empirical work to show that it is typical – a typical Chicago street, say, in terms of the ethnicity and age distribution of its inhabitants – we cannot draw anything meaningful from this typicality in a case study, for the typicality will begin and end with the dimensions by which typicality is framed. We cannot say from having studied this street that its circumstances will have in any way contributed *by their typicality* to the particular situation in which it finds itself (whatever that situation, that 'object' is). We could study the street and be informed about its problems, its tensions, its intrigues, hostilities and kindnesses and while these may in some way be of interest by virtue of the analytical object of the study they would not be of interest by virtue of the street's typicality, since the next typical street would, in terms of such dynamics, in all probability, be very different. In short, the notion of typicality may give an unwarranted impression to any reader that the significance of the analysis rests in the representativeness of the subject. It does not.

The subject is identified, then, in one of three principal ways – as:

- a local knowledge case; or
- a key case; or
- an outlier case.

Objvect

The object is less straightforwardly identified, and, as Ragin (1992) notes, it need not be defined at the outset but, rather, may emerge as an inquiry progresses. Whether it is set at the outset or is emergent, it will be this analytical focus that crystallizes, thickens or develops as the study proceeds: it is the way that this 'object' develops that is at the heart of the study.

Whichever – 'emergent' or set at the outset – it is important to have some notion of a potential object in mind when the study begins and not to confuse it with the subject. As Wieviorka puts it:

> If you want to talk about a 'case', you also need the means of interpreting it or pla-
> cing it in a context ... Regardless of the practical approach for studying it, a case is an
> opportunity of relating facts and concepts, reality and hypotheses. But do not make the
> mistake of thinking that it is, in itself, a concept. (1992: 160)

The object constitutes, then, the analytical frame within which the case is viewed
and which the case exemplifies. For example, in Ball's (1981) case study of a school,
Beachside Comprehensive, the school itself is the subject that exemplifies the analytical frame, the object, which was the process by which change was effected in schools
in the movement to comprehensive education in the UK. Beachside Comprehensive –
the school – was the prism through which 'facts and concepts, reality and hypotheses'
about this change were refracted, viewed and studied.

Becker (in Ragin, 1992) shows how important it is to see the process of employing the object as a dynamic one: as a study proceeds the inquirer should be asking
the question 'What is this a case *of* over and over as evidence accumulates around
potential explanations or 'theories'. Theory is thus *forged* – it is malleable, rather in
the way that Bourdieu talked about theory (in Wacquant, 1989, cited in Jenkins,
1992: 67) being a 'thinking tool'. As Bourdieu put it: '[theory is] a set of *thinking tools*
visible through the results they yield, but it is not built as such ... It is a temporary
construct which takes shape for and by empirical work.' Eckstein (1975: 133) makes
the same point, noting that the theoretical enterprise of case study is not about testing probabilistically stated theories. Rather, it is about discovering or testing tools of
explanation.

The focus on the development of theory in case study is closely linked with
the explication of the analytical object. Bourdieu's emphasis on the theory as tool
therefore reminds us that the elaboration of theory is a means to an end, with
that end being explanation. It is not an end in itself. The development of theory,
whether this be in 'theory-testing' or 'theory-seeking', is central to the dynamic of
the relation between *subject* and *object* in case study and we explore it further in
the next section.

Beyond subject and object: purpose, approach and process

Methodological discourse stresses a number of themes on the direction and organization of case studies – their design – and we summarize some of the better-known
analyses in Table 5.1. Constraint of space prohibits full discussion of all of these,
but we will outline in a little more detail one of the most recent – the analysis from
George and Bennett (2005: 75–6) – for the purposes of explicating the general themes
raised by Table 5.1. Theirs is an especially useful analysis, drawing heavily as it does

on the widely used typologies of Lijphart (1971) and, principally, Eckstein (1975). George and Bennett emerge with six types of case study. These are:

1. *Atheoretical/configurative-idiographic* case studies – that is to say, illustrative studies which do not contribute to theory.
2. *Disciplined configurative* case studies, where established theories are used to explain a case.
3. *Heuristic* case studies wherein new causal paths are identified. Outlier cases may be especially valuable here.
4. *Theory testing* case studies, assessing 'the validity and scope conditions of single or competing theories'.
5. *Plausibility probes* – preliminary studies to determine whether further study is warranted.
6. *'Building block' studies* of particular types, or subtypes 'of a phenomenon, identify common patterns or serve a particular kind of heuristic purpose'.

In the establishment of these six types, a core distinction is being drawn between theoretical and non-theoretical studies and this is a feature of several of the other classifications in Table 5.1. Beyond this, the classification draws attention to illustrative and exploratory studies of one kind or another, as do the other classifications in Table 5.1. Unlike Yin and de Vaus, George and Bennett do not expand their discussion to a further layer of organization: the operationalization of the study – for example, into 'parallel', 'longitudinal' or 'embedded' studies.

Notwithstanding these commonalities and differences, the principal feature to emerge from a listing of this kind is that there is a mixture of criteria for classification. The aim in developing a typology is to synthesize by drawing out strands of commonality while also integrating, where appropriate, classificatory layers and themes – and noting, hopefully to understand, differences. Within and between the commentaries we have selected, purposes are mixed with methods which are mixed with kinds of subject which are in turn mixed with what might be called different operational 'shapes' of case study. These layers of analysis will be examined in turn.

Purpose

There is first a layer of criteria that is about *purpose*. For example, the terms 'intrinsic' and 'instrumental' used by Stake, and the term 'evaluative' as used by Merriam and Bassey, point to a reason for doing the study: its purpose. Likewise, the term 'plausibility probes' used by Mitchell, and George and Bennett points to a purpose – of exploration. And Eckstein uses the term 'heuristic' to refer to exploration; he suggests that heuristic studies can be about arriving at notions of problems to solve. The purpose is intimately connected with the object of the study: the understanding that is required – the explanation that is needed – will be related to the reason for doing the study, that is to say, the purpose.

Table 5.1 Kinds of case studies, as enumerated by different analysts

George and Bennett (2005) (drawing on Eckstein, 1975)	Merriam (1988)	Stake (1995)	Bassey (1999)	de Vaus (2001)	Mitchell (2006) (drawing on Eckstein, 1975)	Yin (2009)
Theory testing	Descriptive	Intrinsic	Theory-seeking	Descriptive/ explanatory	Illustrative	Critical
Atheoretical/ configurative-idiographic	Interpretative	Instrumental	Theory-testing	Theory testing/ theory building	Social analytic	Extreme/unique
Disciplined configurative	Evaluative	Single/collective	Story-telling	Single/multiple case	Extended (over time)	Longitudinal
Heuristic			Picture-drawing	Holistic/embedded	Configurative-idiographic	Represent-ative
Plausibility probes			Evaluative	Parallel/sequential	Disciplined-configurative	Revelatory
'Building block' studies				Retrospective/ prospective	Heuristic	
					Plausibility probes	

Approach and methods

Next, there is the approach that is adopted. It is in this 'layer' that there are the clearest distinctions between kinds of study, reflecting the broad nature of the object and the purpose of the study. Even though those differences exist, a centrality is given in the commentaries to the significance of theory in the conduct of the study, wherein studies that are not in some way theoretical are specifically labelled as such. Thus, in the categorizations of George and Bennett and that of Mitchell (both borrowing from Eckstein), case studies that have no theoretical element are termed 'atheoretical/configurative-idiographic', in part to highlight the illustrative nature of the work in hand. As Lijphart (1971: 691) puts it, these non-theoretical studies '… are entirely descriptive and move in a theoretical vacuum.' Likewise, Bassey makes a distinction between, on the one side, two kinds of theoretical case study (theory-seeking and theory-testing), and on the other those he labels 'picture-drawing' and 'story-telling.'

Thus, one might say that the object of a study may be taken to be, essentially, (i) theoretical or (ii) illustrative. As far as the former is concerned – the theoretical study – the distinction Bassey draws between theory-testing and theory-seeking highlights the different kinds of stance that may be taken about the object: it may be set clearly at the outset (theory-testing), or developed throughout the study (theory-seeking).

After a decision about approach, there are choices to be made about the methods to be adopted. Will the study be entirely interpretative in orientation: will it be an ethnography? Will it use a combination of methods, possibly incorporating experimental (for example, using 'repeated measures' as in Stake's example), survey or cross-sectional elements? Will it involve documentary analysis? Given the methodological pluralism noted earlier, the choices here are abundant. They will, in turn, lead to questions about the operational process of the study – the means by which it is constructed and the means by which the object is understood and refracted through the subject. It is this operational process to which we now turn.

Process

In this classificatory layer, case inquirers are making decisions about the operational processes of their studies. For this, they need first to return to their subjects (as distinct from the object) and to the boundary decisions made at the outset. There has to be an examination of the nature of the choices that were made at that time about the parameters that delimit the subject of the study. These may fall around a number of loci: the case may be defined by one or more of a range of boundary considerations: person, time period, place, event, institution or any of a range of singular phenomena that can be studied in their complexity. The first consideration, though, concerns an important distinction that has been raised by Stake (2005: 445) that will determine the process of the case study, and this is about whether there is to be a comparative element to the study: should it be single or multiple? This single/multiple distinction is at the base of much discussion – and confusion – about the case study, emerging principally from Lijphart's exclusion of what he called (and is still sometimes called) 'comparative research' from the case study family. The latter will be discussed in a moment, after consideration of the central distinction.

Single or multiple

The case study, while it is of the singular, may contain more than one element in its subject and if this is so – that is, if there are two or several cases – each individual case is less important in itself than the comparison that each offers with the others. For example, a study might be conducted of two schools' different capacities for making effective use of a visiting education support service. By contrasting the schools' 'biographies' – their histories, catchments, staff relationships and other characteristics – light would be thrown on the relative dynamics affecting the reception and use of the support service. The key focus would not be on the nature and shape of relationships per se in one school, but rather on the nature of the difference between the one and the other and what this might tell us about the dynamics that were significant in this difference. This comparative element is why Schwandt (2001) calls this kind of case study, *cross-case analysis*.

But one now needs to raise the methodological issue alluded to a moment ago concerning the firm distinction that Lijphart (1971) posited between comparative study and case study. It is a differentiation that has been troubling for subsequent discourse about the nature and 'shape' of case study. Lijphart's influential typology – his six types of case study, distinguished, as they are, from comparative study – presents to us, if we do not read them in the context of four subsequent decades of methodological discussion, some profound misunderstandings. Not many would now agree with Lijphart, for example, that '... the analytical power of the comparative method increases the closer it approximates the statistical and experimental methods' (1971: 693). Lijphart's epistemological stance, disclosed by comments such as this throughout his seminal article, perhaps betrays the methodological tensions existing at the time he was writing (see Alvesson and Sköldberg, 2000 for a discussion). Whatever the reason for his stance, the legacy of his disaggregation of the comparative study from the case study has been confusion about the nature of the case. Suffice it to say that the comparative study is more straightforwardly seen as part of the case study family if one puts the emphasis on *the subject* – which can be singular *or plural* – rather than *the case*.

The boundary and the shape

The choice about single or multiple studies determines what follows in the shape of the case study. Single studies, containing no element of comparison, will take essentially three forms, wherein personal or systemic features of the subject are bounded by time in some shape or form. The case inquirer notices change as it happens and seeks its antecedents and its consequences. We have to find the 'sequence of steps' as Becker puts it (1992: 209) and understand cause in relation to time, with 'each step understood as preceding in time the one that follows it.' In doing this we conjecture not only about how one thing is related to another, but also about how cause and effect change with time as other elements of a situation also change.

We suggest (drawing on other commentators) that the varieties of time-use lead to three kinds of study: *retrospective*, *snapshot* and *diachronic*. The *retrospective* study is the simplest, involving the collection of data relating to a past phenomenon of any kind. The researcher is looking back on a phenomenon, situation, person or event or studying it in its historical integrity. With the *snapshot* the case is being examined in one defined period of time: a current event; a day in the life of a person; a month's diary of a marriage. Whether a month, a week, a day or even a period as short as an hour, the analysis will be aided by the temporal juxtaposition of events. The snapshot develops, the picture presenting itself as a Gestalt over a tight time-frame. The *diachronic* study shows change over time. We use the term 'diachronic' to refer to change over time in preference to the word 'longitudinal' principally to avoid confusion with other kinds of longitudinal research. The essence, though, is the same as that in 'longitudinal': data-capture occurs at points 'a, b, c → n' and one's interest is in the changes occurring at the two or more data collection points.

For multiple studies the researcher considers additional features of the situation. How can the different studies be used for comparison – for cross-case analysis in Schwandt's (2001) terms? There are two principal means of doing this: first by straightforward comparison between clearly different examples, as in Burgess's (1984) ten case studies of research in educational settings, and the contrast between and among the cases throws the spotlight on an important theoretical feature. Second, comparison may be of elements within one case – comparison, in other words, of *nested* elements. With nested studies the breakdown is *within* the principal unit of analysis – for example, wards within a hospital. A nested study is distinct from a straightforwardly multiple study in that it gains its integrity, its wholeness from the wider case. For example, a researcher might be looking at three wards within one hospital, but if the one hospital had no significance other than its physical housing of these three wards then the cases would not be seen as nested. The elements are nested only in the sense that they form an integral part of a broader picture.

A further subdivision may be drawn in the multiple study and this is between parallel and sequential studies. In the former, the cases are all happening and being studied concurrently, while with the sequential study the cases happen consecutively and there is an assumption that what has happened in one or in an intervening period will in some way affect the next.

Integrating the layers: a typology

Having separated the classificatory layers drawn in discourse about case study, we now propose a typology in which they are organized and re-integrated. The typology, incorporating considerations about these layers – concerning subject and object, purpose, approach and process – is summarized in Figure 5.1. While this perhaps implies sequencing to the choices being made, in most cases much of the decision making will in fact occur simultaneously, particularly in relation to the subject, object and approach. The typology offers a 'flattened out' view of the thinking that occurs in the process of research design.

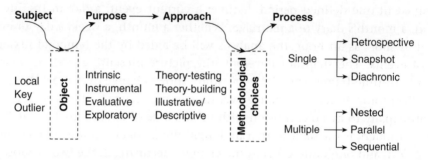

Figure 5.1 A typology of case study

As the typology in a sense 'unrolls' the various considerations being made in the design of a case study it perhaps implies that a series of separate design choices are being made during the planning of the study. So, at first glance it perhaps denies the coherence and simultaneity of the design decisions of which we have just spoken. But for the researcher new to case study the mere existence of these decisions may not have occurred. As a consequence, the variety of design paths will be restricted. A typology encourages a clear articulation of the distinctness and necessity of both subject and object, it encourages consideration of theoretical or illustrative approaches, methodological decisions, and decisions about process: can the research question be addressed by a single focus on one person or situation, or would a comparison be better? Is there a time element that will be addressed by looking at a sequence of events, or is it better to examine one tightly defined period in time? Would it be helpful to extract a number of nested elements from the main focus and to examine these in detail? It is useful to explore all of these considerations alongside thought about subject, object, theory and method.

That last consideration, method, is one that we have not discussed at length in this chapter. It will be discussed in more detail in Chapter 8, where we consider issues of theorization in relation to the discursive elements of the study. Suffice it to say here, though, that methodological considerations will occur throughout the design of the study, remembering that methodological eclecticism is the hallmark of the case study. Case study, as we have been at pains to point out throughout, is not a method in itself. Rather it is a design frame – a scaffold that supports and guides inquiry. Within that scaffold the most appropriate methods for collecting and analyzing data will be employed. Perhaps an ethnographic stance will be taken; perhaps various kinds of observation will be used. A wide variety of methods may be used. The consideration of which will prove most fruitful will be taken in the light of the questions being asked at the outset of the study. That variety of methods is exemplified in some of the examples in Chapter 6, and an even broader selection of methods and epistemological stances is given in Thomas (2013a, 2013b).

Conclusion

The 'weak sibling' status of the case study noted by Yin (2003: xiii) is due at least in part to the uncertainty felt by intending researchers about structure and method. As the design of the case study is presented often as open-ended and untethered – and methodological eclecticism is emphasized in commentary on design – researchers may feel unguided about structure: open-endedness is extended to an unwarranted expectation of structural looseness, and in the absence of a structure that maps out potential routes to follow, important pointers may be missed. We have, therefore, suggested a typology that foregrounds a number of features – classificatory layers – of the study: the distinction between subject and object; the importance of clarifying the purpose of the study; an awareness of the likely analytical approach to be pursued, and an identification of the likely process to be followed in conducting it. By helping to disclose the anatomy of the case study, we hope that the typology will assist in both the construction and analysis of this form of inquiry.

SIX
Working through the typology

The typology given in Chapter 5 reveals that there are numerous valid permutations of the dimensions outlined there and many trajectories therefore open to the case inquirer. Purposes have to be identified first, then approaches need to be delineated (theory-testing, theory-building or illustrative), then processes must be decided upon, with a principal choice being between whether the study is to be single or multiple, and choices also about whether the study is to be retrospective, snapshot or diachronic, and whether it is nested, parallel or sequential. It is thus possible to take many routes through the typology, with, for example, an exploratory, theory-building, multiple, nested study, or, perhaps, an evaluative, theory-testing, single, retrospective study. The typology thus offers many potential avenues for the case inquirer to follow.

This chapter gives ten examples of case studies which take different routes through the typology, as a demonstration of the wide variety of travel which is possible. The diversity in the use of the case study form is also demonstrated by the eclectic selection here, representing a variety of methods of data collection and analysis. To illustrate the extent and breadth of use, we have included not only strictly academic accounts but also accounts which are no less rigorous but which are narrated in a more vernacular style.

Examples: routes through the typology

Example 1: Jared Diamond – how societies survive or fail

Using a set of linked case studies, Diamond (2005) develops a complex thesis about how societies collapse. He looks at a range of communities and societies that have collapsed or are currently in the process of collapsing. The title – *Collapse: How Societies Choose to Fail or Survive* – is the **object** of the research while the **subject** is the set of societies he selects to illuminate and understand the object: today's Montana, Easter Island of the 17th century, Pitcairn, the Mayans, the Vikings, and modern Haiti. Each one is quite different from the others but each is connected to the others by decline and collapse, the object. The theoretical explanation that 'thickens' around the object is that the decline of a society happens because the society's response to change is insufficient to address a range of potential factors, from hostile neighbours to environmental change and degradation.

Let's look in particular at one of Diamond's case studies. Easter Island has always been a mysterious phenomenon to explorers because of its huge, ghostly statues gazing out to sea. Yet today, aside from these striking megaliths, there is virtually nothing there. These sculptures were clearly the product of a centuries-old, highly sophisticated civilization. But why did it evaporate, leaving nothing behind other than these remarkable statues?

Diamond's inquiries consisted of reading widely about the island, using existing research – botanical, cultural, historical – visiting the island for an extended period and working to integrate all of the information that he gathered. He looked at Easter Island's history and geography. He looked at what the people ate, drawing from research using pollen and charcoal remains that gave clues about now-extinct crops. Using archaeological evidence and oral history he looked at the likely structure of the society, at the people's attitudes to death and the after-life, at how the statues might have been sculpted, transported and erected.

Most importantly, he looked at how all of this might be connected in the way that the islanders sought and used resources, from the intensification of their agriculture using windbreaks and pits for better growing, to the division of the island into 11, eventually competing, territories. All of this was pieced together using intelligent questioning and intelligent answering, in a kind of Socratic method, between Diamond himself and an imaginary interlocutor. Here's an example:

> How did all those Easter Islanders, lacking cranes, succeed in carving, transporting, and erecting those statues? Of course we don't know for sure, because no European ever saw it being done to write about it. But we can make informed guesses from oral traditions of the islanders themselves ... from statues in the quarries at successive stages of completion, and from recent experimental tests of different transport methods. (Diamond, 2005: 99)

The method of informed questioning, reasoning and case construction works powerfully. Analysis emerges not just out of the juxtaposition and the combination of inert hard facts (which are, of course, never as hard as we might like them to be) but from a complex chemistry. While he is making his case, Diamond is imagining, linking and connecting ideas. He tells a story and makes a case.

Using the typology, Diamond's was a **multiple** study (since Easter Island was one of several cases) possessing both **subject** and **object**. It involved **key** examples of collapse. It was of **intrinsic** interest, containing **exploratory** elements, and the aim was to explain collapse through **theory-building**. He then wove all of this together using intelligent questioning and answering – essentially, the Socratic method – in the context of the other, **parallel** studies he was collecting to come to a thesis about collapse. While there would have been an integrity to much of the decision-making in this design, an analysis of that decision-making can be displayed as a trajectory through the typology, and this is summarized in Figure 6.1.

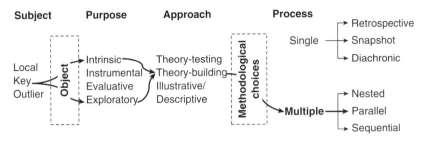

Figure 6.1   Diamond's (2005) study of societal collapse

Example 2: Zigler and Muenchow – the Head Start programme

Our second example is Zigler and Muenchow's (1992) study of the Head Start education programme. It is a much cited study with a clear **subject** (Head Start) but perhaps a less easily identifiable **object**. It is a **local knowledge** case – these were key figures in the programme, co-authoring the presidential report on it. The object could perhaps be said to be the working and the success of the programme, with lessons to be learned, but this is not clearly defined. It is, essentially, a chronicle with observations, analyses of what went right and wrong, and a set of conclusions and recommendations. It is not contextualized, as Wieviorka (1992: 160) puts it, in an 'analytical category or theory' – whether that be expensive national education programmes, attempts at top-down change, the operation of early childhood programmes, or whatever. What *was* it, in other words, that was to be explained? What was the explanandum? The study was essentially **descriptive** and **illustrative** and we can say that via various **methods** – the recollections of the authors, discussions with others and interrogation of official and unofficial records – this was a **single, retrospective** study (see Figure 6.2).

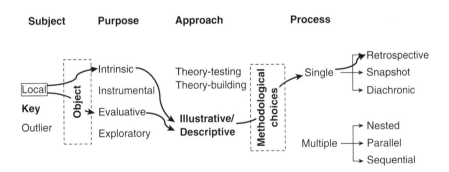

Figure 6.2   Zigler and Muenchow's (1992) study of the Head Start education programme

Example 3:   Peter Johnston – studying reading failure

Johnston (1985), in a paper written for the *Harvard Educational Review*, outlines two different approaches to understanding reading failure. The first is rooted in a belief that people with reading problems process verbal information more slowly than others. The second is that reading problems emerge from 'higher mental processes' such as motivation, or lack of confidence. For this second belief, 'The educational solution ... is to modify or teach learning strategies and discourage the use of ineffective approaches.' By contrast, the first set of beliefs – about neuro-logical dysfunction and processing deficit – 'accepts inappropriate strategies as unchangeable and tries to work around them.'

Johnston notes that what he calls the dominant paradigm in reading research – a 'reductionist approach to the investigation of reading failure' – lends itself to the deficit and neurological explanations and leads to inappropriate analysis of that failure. He argues that 'case studies involving examination of the individual's goals, motives, and situations should play a much larger role in research into reading failure.'

He goes on to argue that the case study is the most appropriate way to look at reading failure. Cognitive strategies are individual, and because the case study recognizes individual diversity, these strategies are best studied through case study processes. He notes that there has, however, been little employment of its benefits over the history of education research. (He was writing in 1985, but the same is true today, in the 21st century.) He proceeds:

> With few exceptions (for example, see Coles, 1987), cognitive scientists in the field of reading have not accepted case studies as sources of data for expanding theory and practice. *Reading Research Quarterly*, the major research journal in the field, has not published a single case study in its entire history. This amounts to a gross imbalance in methodology. (Johnston, 1985: 155)

For several reasons, then, Johnston chose to examine reading failure through the use of case study. He decided to work with adult disabled readers rather than younger disabled readers because of an important advantage: they have more conscious access to the thinking processes involved in reading than do young children with difficulties in reading. They are able to talk about these and reflect on them.

He took a theory-first approach to his study. This was that:

> ... reading disability results from a combination of conceptual difficulties, rational and irrational use of self-defeating strategies, and negative affective responses. ... Employing Vygotsky's (1978) perspective on psychological research, I will argue that an understanding of reading failure cannot be gained through fragmented analyses of the speed of performance of various isolated mental acts out of the context of their social and motivational environment and antecedents. Rather, a useful understanding will only emerge from an integrated examination of the cognitive, affective, social, and personal history of the learner. (Johnston, 1985: 155)

Elucidating and illuminating this theme was the **object** of his research.

Three adult men were selected – Bill, Jack and Charlie – to be the **subjects** of the case study. They had great difficulty in reading, even though they were all employed in good, secure jobs. Their reading was at kindergarten (nursery), second grade (Y2) and third grade (Y3) levels.

The work with these men involved individual sessions which were tape-recorded. Eight sessions ranging from 45 minutes to two hours were recorded. The sessions involved interactive assessment, spontaneous and elicited introspection and retrospection, and think-aloud reports and oral reading performance. Other methods, which involved tracking out-loud reading involving the evidence from audio recordings, were also used.

Findings centred on the strategies used by the men as they were reading, involving:

> ... misconceptions or missing conceptions about various aspects of reading. A minor but interesting example is Bill's pronunciation of 'dwindle' as 'windle'. Did he simply not see the first letter? When asked to repeat it and explain, he noted that the *d* looked as though it ought to be silent. Another example is that Charlie was unable to perform phonemic segmentation of words. (Johnston, 1985: 157)

Johnston also gained retrospective accounts from the men of the coping strategies they had used. For example:

Bill: Through first and second grade I can remember memorizing the books. I didn't read the stories, I would memorize them.

P. J. [Peter Johnston]: Did you know that wasn't really reading?

Bill: No.

P. J.:   Or did you think that was what it was all about?

Bill: At the time, yes.

(Johnston, 1985: 157)

He went on to draw inferences from this:

> Suppose that intelligent individuals such as Bill, Jack, and Charlie developed the notion that reading is largely remembering. They may continue to be at least moderately successful until the second or third grade, by which time the materials would be too difficult for them. To reveal their ignorance at that point would be socially stressful. Additionally, because the erroneous beliefs sometimes seem related to success, they are difficult to give up, much the same way that gambling beliefs and behaviors are difficult to erase. (Johnston, 1985: 157)

The remaining analysis conducted by Johnston is fascinating, relying on his interpretations of the men's errors and his exploration of the strategies used to cope with not being able to read. For example, there is this question and answer exchange, again with Bill. Bill encountered the word *Charlene*, his thinking went as follows:

Bill: Charlotte – Charlene [long pause].

P. J.:   Is it Charlotte or Charlene? How would you know? How would you figure it out?

Bill: It's Charlene?

P. J.:   How did you know?

Bill: Because I have a Charlene ... ah ... working for me at work.

P. J.:   OK. But how would you be able to figure it out from the letters?

Bill: l-e-n-e /eˉn/ it looks to me.

P. J.:   What would Charlotte end with?

Bill: e-t.

(Johnston, 1985: 162)

Johnston notes that Bill's particular weakness, the text-driven strategies, are avoided even when they are available. He concludes that Bill's problem is 'strategic rather than neurological'.

An interesting analysis occurs when, in order to examine how the men were using strategies to avoid looking carefully at words, a masking device comprising a piece of cardboard with a hole in it was used to restrict their view. Using this, together with a taped record of when they spoke (i.e. when they read out-loud), it was possible to see how their utterance related to what they were looking at. The findings are recorded in Figure 6.3. Johnston concludes that the substantial hesitations made at several points seem to be down to interference between the demands of voice production and decoding.

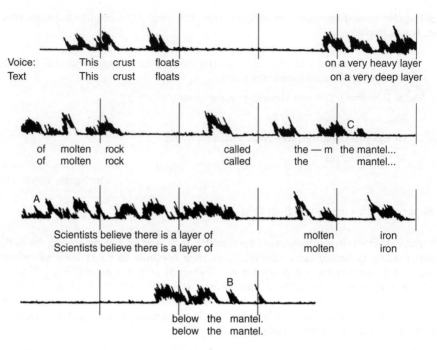

Voice: This crust floats   on a very heavy layer
Text   This crust floats   on a very deep layer

of molten rock   called   the — m the mantel...
of molten rock   called   the   mantel...

Scientists believe there is a layer of   molten   iron
Scientists believe there is a layer of   molten   iron

below the mantel.
below the mantel.

Figure 6.3 Voice print showing the location and extent of pauses between words as read by Bill

Note: When Bill's voice is at point A, his attention is already focused on point B. Similarly, his attention is focused on point C some time before his voice arrives at the point. The substantial hesitations preceding points B and C (the problematic word 'mantel') are apparently caused by interference between the demands of voice production and decoding.

Problems were also caused by anxiety, as evidenced by Jack's account:

> *Jack*: What it is, it's the old feelings. It's like, y'know, well … something will trigger it. Like when I was a kid in school and they would ask me the first day, I would be in a first … say, a new class, and they would ask me to read, and the teacher didn't know that I couldn't read. Well, those feelings still can come back to me, and it's like a feeling … never … I can't even begin to explain. It's like you completely feel isolated, totally alone, and when that sets in … course, I don't get it now like I did then … but it's still that quaint feeling will come over me, and if I … if it overwhelms me … it … it … it takes you right up … you know, and you do, you shut right down. (Johnston, 1985: 167)

Other causes of failure were put down to motivation, goals and personal attributions for the failure. The men seemed to be in cycles of inappropriate decoding strategies, anxiety and self-blame from which they could not escape. The insights for what happens to children at school are legion and the analysis, gathered from a range of sources and methods, does much to confirm the theoretical explanation proposed by the researcher at the outset.
    Johnston concludes that:

> Most current explanations of reading difficulties focus on the level of operations, devoid of context, goals, motives, or history. … Until we can integrate the depth of human

feeling and thinking into our understanding of reading difficulties, we will have only a shadow of an explanation of the problem and ill-directed attempts at solutions. (Johnston, 1985: 174)

One can put the analysis undertaken by this researcher into the taxonomy as shown in Figure 6.4.

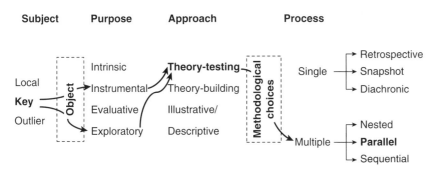

Figure 6.4 Johnston's (1985) study of reading failure

The **subjects** of the study were the three men. The **object** was to elucidate the analytical frame outlined – a Vygotskian position that the social context for individuals' reading failure is more important than any supposed cognitive deficits. The subjects were **key cases** – not in this instance well-known or notorious cases, but key cases identified by the researcher – where the purpose was **instrumental** and **exploratory** and the approach was to **test a theory** (that theory being that reading failure is attributable more to failure in strategy than neurological dysfunction). The researcher used a wide range of methods, from audio taping to visual tracking, from observation to interviews. He used **multiple** cases, but these were not comparative in any significant way; rather, they were **parallel** to each other.

Example 4: John C. Caldwell – puzzling longevity in Kerala

Caldwell (1986) was interested in the factors that might affect development in less developed societies. How could societies break out of cycles of poverty and high infant mortality? This was the **object** of his study. He began by examining the correlation between gross national product per head in a country and the average life expectancy of a person in that country. He was looking at the association of average income with the age a person could be expected to live. A high correlation was expected and revealed: as income goes up, so life expectancy should go up. Caldwell's great inspiration was to focus on the exceptions – countries (or states within countries) which bucked the trend, which were outliers.

A shining outlier is the Indian state of Kerala. This became his **subject**. The state has extremely low levels of income – at the time Caldwell's study was done it had a gross domestic product per person of $160, which placed it higher than only four other countries in the entire world. Despite this, it had life expectancy of 66 years, well up with the best performers including industrialized states in the West. How could this be explained? Caldwell's focus was on how Kerala and two other similar outlier states, Sri Lanka and Costa Rica, achieved such good life expectancy and whether similar routes could be followed by others.

Looking back to the original statistics, which came from a Rockefeller Foundation inquiry, Caldwell noted that the inquiry's author had suggested that Kerala's achievements had come through a combination of 'political and social will'. He was left with a series of questions, which included the following:

- In what ways do countries with exceptionally good health records contrast with those with exceptionally bad ones?
- Under what circumstances can political and social will be exercised? To what extent has the political leadership been uniquely shaped by the history and nature of its society?
- For countries with vastly different histories from those with success stories, are there lessons to be learned or policies that can be put in place to accelerate mortality reduction?

His research design route in answering these questions was to conduct a case inquiry. He had to use available statistics, knowledge of culture and history to arrive at potential explanations about why Kerala, Sri Lanka and Costa Rica had been able to manage such extraordinary accomplishments in the health and longevity of their citizenry.

The first job he set himself was to isolate from the statistics not just the best but also the worst, to see if this offered any opportunity for contrast. In doing this, he was struck by what appeared to be a cultural difference between the best achievers and the worst achievers. The worst achievers happened to be Oman, Saudi Arabia and Iran, with incomes 15 times higher than the poor states with good life expectancy, yet life expectancy only down in the 50s. What could be different between the achievements of Kerala, Sri Lanka and Costa Rica on the one hand, and Oman, Saudi Arabia and Iran on the other?

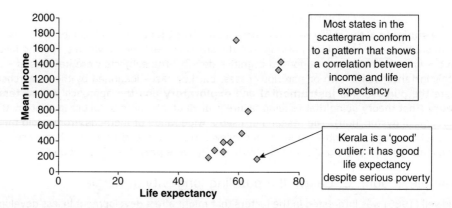

Figure 6.5 Life expectancy in years against mean income ($)

Caldwell hypothesized that cultural and religious differences were at the root of many of the differences between these two groups of states. In the cases of Kerala and Sri Lanka the Buddhist tradition stresses 'enlightenment', which can be interpreted in Western terms as education. By contrast, the rich poor-achievers – Oman, Saudi Arabia and Iran – were characterized by cultural and religious traditions that separated women, giving them limited access to education. Not only were there low levels of female schooling in these countries, but also low levels of family planning and limited access to employment for women outside the household. The link with female education is striking, notes Caldwell: 'For most countries in both lists the 1982 infant mortality rankings are very close to the 1960 female primary school enrolment rankings' (1986: 177): as education of females goes up, infant mortality goes down.

He concludes that there are some remarkable parallels between these states:

These parallels include a substantial degree of female autonomy, a dedication to education, an open political system, a largely civilian society without a rigid class structure, a history of egalitarianism and radicalism and of national consensus arising from political contest. (Caldwell, 1986: 182)

In a fascinating and wide-ranging analysis, Caldwell suggests reasons for the importance of the position of women in society, from the likelihood of girls becoming nurses to the position of children in society being higher where that of women is higher. He drew on the work of a 19th-century anthropologist, John Davy, who had noted that the Sinhalese treated their children with 'extraordinary affection' attending to them when sick in the way that other groups he had studied had not.

Caldwell's conclusion was that the women's education may be important not just because women may know more about, say, nutrition and development for babies, but also because women are valued and included – something more intangible but nonetheless seemingly just as significant. Thus, the provision of education for all seems to be operating at two levels: it is providing for individual knowledge, but it is also symbolic of society's affirmation of once-marginalized groups, and its endorsement of those groups' participation and inclusion. So in some way this provision seems to be endowing added value. Perhaps this value-added comes in the form of a boost for identity, status, belonging and self-belief. Inclusion, and the status it brings, breeds not only health but also the conditions for learning and growth to occur.

He looks also at historical and cultural investment in health and hygiene, noting that the high performers had a record of valuing these areas and investing powerfully in them right back to the 19th century. Education is important, too, but not just as education per se. It is linked with an active and participatory political system that in some way enables the hearing of the people's 'voice'. Caldwell puts it thus:

> All evidence suggests that continuing political activity is important, especially if there is a dominant populist or radical element, and that such activity hastens the emergence and the spreading throughout the community of adequate educational and health systems. However, such politics are often encouraged by educating the electorate, and this has an impact at the grass-roots as well as at the upper level. (Caldwell, 1986: 203)

He compares this with what happens elsewhere in India: 'The inefficiency of much of the health infrastructure in rural India is explained by both the low educational levels and the political passivity of the poor' (p. 203). There appears to be a symbiosis between education and health.

Although Caldwell's work is at no point called a case study, it emphatically is one – of this limited set of countries. In doing work with such a small number he cannot definitively assert that factor x or factor y is the cause of the good life-expectancy figures in these outlier countries, but he can have a good, informed guess. And this guess can be buttressed with evidence from historical records, from other statistics, from anthropological studies, from reasoning about cultural difference. In fact, while Caldwell's study starts off as an epidemiological inquiry based largely on statistics it ends more as a comparative history. The inclusion of all of the forms of data, argument, reasoning and analysis is a form of triangulation that should not be downplayed in importance. The outlier case is always a puzzle, and Caldwell amasses all of this evidence – he brings together Foucault's 'polyhedron of intelligibility' – to emerge with intelligent potential solutions – informed guesses – about the puzzle.

Such informed guesses are examples of the abduction (after Peirce, 1992 [1878]) we spoke of in Chapter 4 – a kind of reasoning which, it was argued there, seems particularly apposite for social science. It is an example of 'inference to the best explanation' (Harman; 1965; Lipton; 1991). So, to call such thinking 'informed guessing' is perhaps to underplay its significance and power, for the use of informed guessing is the foundation stone of good analysis. As long as it involves the intelligent putting together of evidence it provides the basis for solution finding and problem solving.

It is worth noting that if Caldwell's study were undertaken today the inquirer would be able to draw on a wider range studies that have used Kerala, as he did, as an example of an extraordinary, outlier phenomenon. For example, the Nobel Prize-winning economist Amartya Sen (1999: 45–8) describes the process operating in Kerala as a 'support-led' approach to improvement in life conditions: 'The support-led process does not operate through fast economic growth, but works through a program of skilful social support of health care, education and other relevant social arrangements.' The inquirer could draw upon Sen's notion of 'capability' among a nation's citizenry, which he takes to be more important than imposed top-down measures designed for the good of the people. In other words, this is about giving the people the opportunity to be involved – a concept similar to the one Caldwell identified in the participatory political system.

Figure 6.6 shows Caldwell's case study in terms of the taxonomy. Kerala was, for Caldwell, an outlier case: it was a conspicuous example of an unusual phenomenon. From it, he wished to explore the evidential territory and try to understand the nature of the puzzling longevity found in the people of Kerala. In doing this, his purpose was instrumental: he wished to find out for a particular reason – the purpose was not, in other words, open-ended. The approach, however – in the context of the study's object (namely circumstances which could lead to development) – was theory-building; although he presumably had ideas in his mind when he undertook the study, he did not set out with the intention of testing a theory about the issue; rather, he sought to build explanations based on the evidence he gathered. Again, this was an example of inference to the best explanation. His process was to use a single, retrospective study – looking at one case in detail and to do this retrospectively by examining official statistics, documentary analysis and existing academic commentary on the phenomenon.

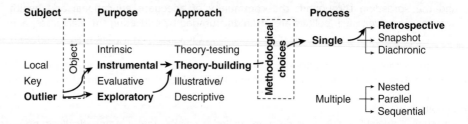

Figure 6.6   Caldwell's (1986) study of puzzling longevity

Example 5: Bryant and Monk – examining the origins of BSE

This example comes from the arena of public health protection. After the arrival of bovine spongiform encephalopathy, or BSE ('mad cow disease'), in the UK in the 1980s, it was realized after laboratory work that the disease had been transferred to the cows from ground-up sheep (including their brains), which had been fed to the cattle as bonemeal. Because the cows were by nature herbivores, the eventual assumption about their infection was that they had no evolutionary protection from the diseases that might be transferred by eating another creature. A collateral assumption was that the new disease, found to be caused by an agent called a 'prion' in the cows' brains, could not be transferred to humans (we being omnivores and thus, the presumption being, possessing some evolution-based protection from eating dangerous parts of other animals).

Not long after the appearance of BSE among cattle it was noted that the incidence of a human brain disease called Creutzfeld-Jakob Disease was rising. It was a particular kind of

Creutzfeld-Jakob Disease – a variant, and the new illness came to be called *variant Creutzfeld-Jakob Disease* or vCJD for short. Eventually, the link between BSE and vCJD was established – BSE seemed to be causing vCJD – but the mechanism for transfer from cattle to humans was unclear and it was expected that the risk of getting the disease was tiny.

In 2000, though, it was noted that alongside the rising incidence of vCJD there was a cluster of people with vCJD in the Leicestershire village of Queniborough. Between August 1996 and January 1999, five people had contracted the disease (and all subsequently died). This was now a huge concern for public health: could it be that this was the beginning of an epidemic? Was it possible that everyone in the country who had eaten beef was susceptible to contracting vCJD? The cluster had to be investigated quickly to explore if there were particular circumstances that were causing this cluster, and if many more clusters were likely to be found across the nation.

The only form of investigation possible here was case study. This case, defined by this cluster, had to be explored for the circumstances that surrounded it. Were there peculiar circumstances in Queniborough that led to the vCJD cluster? Two researchers, Gerry Bryant and Philip Monk (2001), led the investigation for Leicestershire Health Authority and their research provides for us a classic exploratory case study, with the aim – the object – of discovering mechanisms of transmission.

A number of lines of thought were open to the investigators. Aside from the unwelcome possibility that this was the first of many such clusters to appear, there were also competing explanatory themes that had to be explored. The disease had a long incubation and the young adults affected had probably contracted it several years previously, at primary school. Might hygiene in the primary school kitchen be to blame? Might a particularly badly infected batch of cattle be responsible? Was it something to do with the slaughter of the cattle or the transport of the meat? Yet more potential explanations open to Bryant and Monk included the following: (i) infection through blood transfusions, dental surgery, injections, body piercing, etc.; (ii) baby foods (given the ages of the vCJD patients); (iii) lack of manganese in the diet: preliminary investigation showed that this area of Leicestershire has a low level of

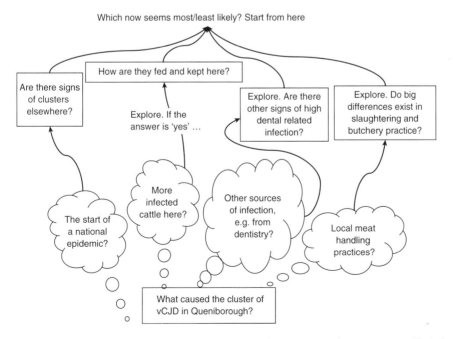

Figure 6.7 Generating ideas is a haphazard process. Follow the ones that seem most likely first

manganese in the soil – could manganese elsewhere be providing some kind of protection? Any of these lines of thought could provide a promising avenue to pursue ... or could lead to a dead-end – the potential routes for inference to the best explanation are given in Figure 6.7.

The investigators had to think about the alternatives given in Figure 6.7 and start with the most likely. They started by looking into cattle-rearing practices locally. They found that, 'Local beef cattle were raised alongside dairy cattle. This meant that beef cattle were fed meat and bonemeal supplements from the age of 6 days rather than 6 months, which is the case for pure beef herds.' The upshot was that the cattle raised here had a higher chance of incubating BSE, having had a longer exposure to the prion in bonemeal than in many places elsewhere, and this area of Leicestershire did indeed prove to have a high incidence of BSE.

A strong additional candidate for culpability was the nature of the meat eaten in this particular place, which leads the investigative trail to butchers' shops. It transpired that butchers in the area obtained their carcasses in one of three ways: they slaughtered the animals themselves; they bought from local small slaughterhouses; or they bought from large wholesale suppliers. So the investigators also looked in more detail at the differing cattle-slaughtering practice in each place. They discovered that the local practice in small slaughterhouses included the insertion of a 'pithing rod' after the cattle were killed with a bolt. The pithing rod is pushed through the bolt-hole in the brain of the cow to prevent the animal kicking, which can occur after the use of the bolt. This practice is not used in large slaughterhouses (and the practice has now been made illegal). There were two other major differences:

- In large 'industrial' slaughterhouses carcasses were hosed down after killing, while in the smaller ones they were, by contrast, wiped, because by the lore of traditional butchery, hosing made the meat 'go sour'.
- Traditional practice employed by the small local slaughterhouses and butchers had been to split the head to remove the brain, offering further opportunity for cross-infection; this practice was not used in the large slaughterhouses.

Local killing and butchering practices, then, provided a likely candidate for infection. They could actually be responsible for spilling infective agent out of the brains of the cattle and onto raw meat. Using the traditional butchers' methods this would not be hosed away. In fact, the use of cloths to wipe the carcasses could actually make matters worse by spreading around the infective agent.

Following their initial investigations, Bryant and Monk refined their original 'inference to best explanation' ideas (see Figure 6.7) to arrive at a hypothesis that:

a) local cattle were particularly predisposed to being infected because in local rearing practice consumption of bonemeal happened at an early age; and ...
b) ... then, the infective agent was spread over carcasses by the local slaughtering and
butchering practices. From there, the infective agent was transferred to butchers' local
customers. (It was known from experimental work that the infective agent – the prion –
is not destroyed by cooking, in the way that other pathogens are destroyed.)

They tested the second part of this hypothesis by comparing the source of meat consumed by vCJD patients and that of non-patients. Was there a pattern, with the families of patients with vCJD sourcing their meat from traditional local butchers? Using a structured questionnaire, they first of all asked relatives of the infected patients about diet and purchasing of meat during the 1980s. The responses here were compared with those of a set of 'controls': the latter were comparable people who had not contracted vCJD.

The findings were, in short, that four of the five vCJD casualties had regularly consumed meat from one of two local butchers which had sourced their meat from cattle killed using traditional slaughtering methods. The meat bought by the controls was from a far wider range of retailers (supermarkets, freezer stores and other butchers). These 'safe' retailers were questioned about the source of their meat, which turned out, as expected, *not* to have been butchered using the traditional methods.

Using simple statistics it was possible to show that the likelihood of this pattern occurring by chance was very slim indeed. However, the point made in Chapter 3 about the difficulty of generalizing from case study is still valid, and Bryant and Monk, the investigators, are wisely cautious in their conclusions. They say that the study '... provides a biologically plausible explanation ... [and] On a national basis, it is unlikely to explain how all of the people who have developed this disease were exposed to the BSE agent'.

However, enormously helpful information had been provided by this case study. An unexpected additional piece of information came from this study – to quote the investigators: 'Analysis of the exposure of our cases to this butchering practice points to an incubation period for the development of variant Creutzfeld-Jakob Disease of between ten and sixteen years. This is the first time that it has been possible to provide an estimate of the incubation period'.

This case study is from the field of public health, but the steps taken by these investigators in doing this exploratory work are common to all such investigations, in any field. They involve:

- initial fieldwork, or reconnoitre, for gathering facts;
- the posing of potential explanations or solutions;
- exploratory work to examine the likelihood of any of those potential explanations having substance; and
- the testing of those potential explanations.

The case here fits in to the typology as shown in Figure 6.8.

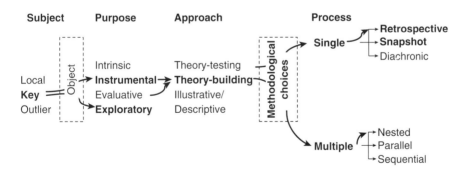

Figure 6.8 Bryant and Monk's (2001) study of transfer of BSE to humans

Queniborough, the **subject**, was, in other words, a **key** case: it provided a conspicuous instance of the phenomenon in question, and one which urgently needed to be studied. It was both **exploratory** and **instrumental**, as with the other studies reviewed. There was no pre-established theory which needed to be tested. Rather, it was a question of **building and eliminating theories** as they seemed to arise in light of the evidence which emerged – theories which would help to throw light on the **object**, namely means of transmission of the disease in humans. The case study could be said to be both **single** and **multiple**. It was single in the sense that this was one phenomenon being studied in detail; it had integrity and coherence in itself and needed to be studied as such. However, there were also multiple elements given that the study had to examine the cases of a number of individual vCJD patients. Each of these, it was assumed, was related within the small geographical nexus of the disease outbreak: it was assumed that this nexus provided a reason for the intensity of outbreak in this locality. There was absolute eclecticism in the choice of **methods** used to address the questions raised: primary school records, investigation of butchery practices, examination of records about incubation periods for the disease. All available knowledge was, in other words, gathered, collated and reviewed with a view to coming to the 'best explanation'.

Example 6: Rageh Omaar – what breeds 'intelligence'?

This example is a case study undertaken by the investigative journalist Rageh Omaar. In a television film about race and intelligence, Omaar started with a set of puzzling and troubling findings about race and achievement. In essence, his study concerned the significantly worse performance at school of young people who are Black and Hispanic than those who are Caucasian. It's a well-established phenomenon. But why should it occur? This was his prima facie question – the **object** of his study.

Omaar first outlined traditional explanations for this poor achievement. Intelligence was (and is often still) taken to be at the root of achievement. He looked back through psychological accounts for differences in intelligence, being able to locate a powerful stream of thought in the early 20th century which had settled on a supposedly hereditary basis for differences in ability. At that time there was a keen desire to calibrate people's abilities and this found its expression in the development of intelligence testing and the IQ test. All this happened at roughly the same time as a flowering of interest in Darwin's ideas, summed up in the idea of 'the survival of the fittest'. This came to be used by 'social-Darwinists', in a terrible distortion of the theory of evolution, as an argument for sterilizing people of lesser ability, in a movement which came to be known as eugenics (see Thomas and Loxley, 2007).

Although eugenics and the social Darwinism on which it is based are now objectionable, their legacy resides in a strong undercurrent of belief about the heritability of intelligence. This is still at the core of many people's attitude to success and failure. Omaar interviewed some key psychologists who took this view. The attitude they hold extends to beliefs about differential intelligence among different ethnic groups, with the assumption that people of Black and Hispanic ethnic origin tend to be of lower intelligence than Whites and Asians.

Omaar's study was now beginning to take shape: he was able to refine his research questions with the benefit of new ideas. One of the ideas he took forward was that of the so-called 'Flynn effect'. James R. Flynn is a researcher who has noted that intelligence, which is supposed to stay fairly stable both in individuals and in populations, is in fact rising. The rise is disguised by the fact that IQ scores always stay at 100. This resolute maintenance of the score at 100 happens because of a standard practice in psychometric science, which involves a periodic 're-normalization' of the data from which IQ scores are calculated.

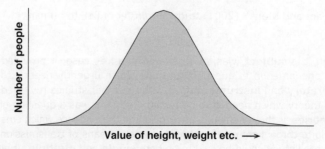

Figure 6.9 The normal distribution curve

IQ construction is based on the idea that the values of most variables – height, weight, etc. – are normally distributed. In other words, there are most occurrences in the middle of the range (e.g. there are most people of average height) with relatively few occurrences at either end of the range (i.e. relatively few people who are very tall or very short). In between are intermediate numbers of people, and the distribution can be graphed to produce the curve shown in Figure 6.9. This 'normal distribution curve' describes the way in which most attributes in nature are dispersed among a population and the assumption among the early psychologists was that this should also be the case for the phenomenon they labelled 'intelligence'.

This assumption about normal distribution is all very well for height and weight, which are unproblematically measured, but things are rather more complicated in the social sciences, and as far as intelligence is concerned we cannot just measure it with a ruler or weighing scales. In fact, the idea of intelligence has been *constructed* – it's made up – and in its construction, because of the assumption that intelligence is a normally distributed phenomenon, there has had to be a correction of the raw scores people get on tests to produce revised scores ('standardized scores') that conform to the normal distribution curve. The standardized scores make it look as though what people are achieving is normally distributed and, because of normalization, that this distribution is staying constant over time.

Flynn (1987) showed, with an article called 'Massive IQ gains in 14 nations: what IQ tests really measure' (and his later work: Flynn, 1998, 1999, 2003; Dickens and Flynn, 2001) that 'intelligence' was not stable if you go back to the pre-normalized, raw figures. People's ability to do 'thinking tasks' is rising.

Interest in Flynn's work has centred on why the rise should be taking place, but more interesting, certainly as far as Omaar's developing research question was concerned, is the light that it throws on the construct of intelligence. If intelligence is not the stable, normally distributed phenomenon it was once thought to be, it cannot be used as the basis for explanations about why people of different ethnicity fare better or worse at school. It is more satisfactory to use the far simpler explanation that we get better at the things we practise. If our lives at home give us no practice in the things that are demanded of us at school then we are almost bound to do less well there. Given that Black and Hispanic children are disproportionately from poor families where there is likely to be less of that kind of school-related activity going on, the explanation for their poorer performance can be seen straightforwardly in such terms.

This literature review of this theoretical background provided the backdrop for the case that Omaar was making – a theory-building and picture-drawing case about the influence that school can have in countering expectations about achievement. He could reformulate his prima facie question to a completely new one: 'What influence can school have in countering expectations about achievement?' In answering this, he would need to draw on the analysis conducted as part of his literature review, and he would draw also on empirical work: the case study.

Omaar's next step was to identify a school that had bucked the trend – an outlier case that had shown that a catchment of entirely Black and Hispanic children could achieve extraordinary feats given favourable circumstances at school. The school he chose – his **subject** – was Hostos-Lincoln Academy of Science in the Bronx, New York. This is one of the poorest and toughest areas in America, with 80 per cent of its students eligible for free or reduced-price lunch programmes.

Hostos-Lincoln Academy is one of 36 schools in its locale. It is a public school (i.e. a state school) that serves 534 students in the secondary school grades 6–12. All of its students are Black (23 per cent), Hispanic (73 per cent) or of Asian/Pacific island origin (4 per cent). Despite the problems of poverty and deprivation, Hostos-Lincoln Academy is getting its students into some of the best colleges in America. This achievement cannot be explained by better resourcing, for the school has 17 students for every teacher, whereas the average for New York is 13 students per teacher.

Assessment results show just how well the school is doing with its students: 52 per cent of the school's students met or exceeded standards in English Language while the average for schools in the same district of New York is 31 per cent. In maths, 77 per cent of Hostos-Lincoln Academy students met or exceeded standards while the average in the district was 51 per cent. In science, 38 per cent of students met or exceeded standards while the average for schools in the district was 29 per cent. Achievement was similar in all subjects: social studies, chemistry, Earth science, living environment, etc.

But this demonstration of difference is not what is at the heart of this case study. Just to show that the school is different is of no interest without what follows. The heart of the research is in the in-depth analysis of what happens in the school to achieve the results it achieves. Omaar concentrated on what was going on in the school to enable it to help its young people so effectively. He interviewed the principal of the school, Nicholas Paarlberg, visited classrooms, made observations, talked to students and teachers, and took particular interest in one 13 year old student, who became a nested case within the larger one of the school.

Omaar's conclusions relate to high expectations, to affirmation, and to students being given access to culture outside their own. When the students graduated they were allowed a part of the main corridor wall to write their name on to show that they had graduated. In the nested case study of the student, Kwan, Omaar showed that Kwan resided in a tiny one-bed apartment where he lived, ate and slept, but at Hostos he was 'transported to another world, and he is thriving on it'.

Omaar linked important elements to produce a well-integrated case study. He had:

1. noticed something worth investigating, namely the consistently poor performance of Black and Hispanic students at school;
2. developed a theory as to why this should be;
3. looked to find a counter example, or outlier case where the usual state of affairs (i.e. the poor performance of these students) did not obtain;
4. undertaken a case study of the outlier case by which he sought to explain the better performance of the Black and Hispanic students in this case in the context of the theory he had developed on the basis of his reading; and
5. used the case study both as an explanation and as an illustration.

His work was multi-layered as far as the typology is concerned (see Figure 6.10), serving different purposes and taking different approaches. Its route through the typology is given in Figure 6.10. Given his starting point – about the provenance and place of the notion of intelligence – he had to conduct contextualization via the relevant literature to build a potential theory which he would then test using his case study. The theoretical position which he built, on the basis of the work of Flynn and others, was that the idea of intelligence had been misleading: it had led to the belief that it was genetically fixed and that there was little that schools (or other cultural institutions) could do to counter its effects. His **object** was to throw light on this. His identification of a **subject** therefore rested on the ability of that subject to contradict standard explanations resting in intelligence. That identification came in the discovery of Hostos-Lincoln Academy, an **outlier** to the general rule that schools succeed in relation to their student intake. Not only was a **theory developed and tested** by the case study, it also served as a powerful illustration for Omaar's purposes as a researcher and a journalist. The study was a **single** one, taking a **snapshot** of the Academy as Omaar visited it and also looking at its history, its mission and its records and at the official statistics of its environs and the other local schools – looking at it, in other words, **retrospectively**. There were **nested** elements to this in the particular focus on one of the school's students. The **methods** Omaar chose to use included interview, observation and examination of local, national and school records.

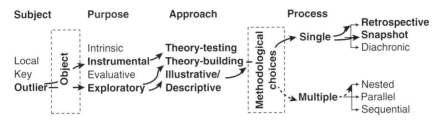

Figure 6.10 Omaar's (2009) case study of Hostos-Lincoln Academy

Example 7: Richard Sennett – sharing craft knowledge

This case study comes from Richard Sennett's book *The Craftsman* (2009) – a highly readable work of scholarship about craft knowledge, how it is acquired and how it is passed on to others. It demonstrates a point Sennett makes about the ways in which a mentor shares knowledge with an apprentice. The point he is trying to convey is, he says, 'Show, don't tell'. In other words, in helping to share a craft with another person – whether it is woodworking, cooking or whatever – the 'instructor', mentor or expert should give examples rather than trying to explain. It doesn't matter how strange the examples are; they are better than instructions based on task analysis. The mind doesn't work like a computer, with watertight sequences of 'do this; don't do that; now do this'. Human beings (as distinct from computers) need real examples from life which they can get inside and occupy. The lesson is that metaphors from practice are better than instructions. We learn by empathizing, imagining and doing, feeling our way with the guidance of a tutor. Whether this tutor is a real flesh and blood person or whether it is a book is immaterial. What is needed is the feeling that the learner is sharing the task, understanding its lineaments and interstices, being guided rather than being told. For those familiar with the psychology of learning, the congruence with Vygotsky's thinking is clear. Forms of effective communication constitute the **object** of his study.

In order to illustrate his point, he identifies four chefs – his subject. He compares them, focusing on the ways that they communicate the means by which they prepare and cook their own special chicken recipes. Sennett's case study is:

- a local knowledge case, emerging from his own experience;
- instrumental, since it serves a purpose;
- illustrative, since it is showing something;
- theory-building, since the illustration leads to discussion, which leads in turn to analysis; and
- multiple/parallel, since the core of the analysis emerges from the comparison of cases.

Sennett legitimately uses a panoply of different sources for compiling his thesis: historical records, case studies, conversations, reminiscences, personal experiences, scientific literature, and more.

The first chef Sennett describes is Richard Olney. Sennett picks on his description of how to bone a chicken. The instructions provided by Olney are less than helpful, says Sennett, because they *tell* instead of showing. As Sennett puts it: 'If the reader already knows how to bone, this description might be a useful review; for the neophyte it is no guide. Many unfortunate chickens will be hacked to bits if a beginner follows it'.

Here is a sample of the instructions that Sennett is talking about: 'Sever the attachment of each shoulder blade at the wing joint and, holding it firmly between the thumb and forefinger of the left hand, pull it out of the flesh with the other hand ...' He likens this kind of writing to engineering: 'Not only do engineer-writers leave out "dumb things"

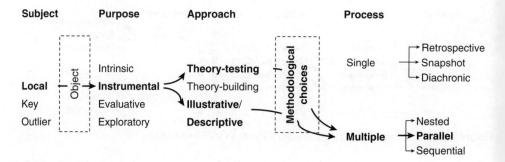

Figure 6.11 Sennett's (2009) case study of sharing craft knowledge

that "everyone knows": they repress simile, metaphor, and adverbial color. The act of unpacking what's buried in the vault of tacit knowledge can make use of these imaginative tools.'

The second part of the multiple case study comes in a word-picture that Sennett draws of chef Julia Child. He gives an account of how Child's recipe is like a story that gets inside the chef's head, expressing forebodings and sympathy. She uses analogy, focusing on the cook rather than on the chicken. She gives clues rather than direct instructions and she guides the reader like an expert with an apprentice, anticipating difficulties and suggesting ways around them: '... for a moment Child will imagine holding the knife awkwardly; the cello master will return to playing wrong notes. This return to vulnerability is the sign of the sympathy the instructor gives.'

Part three is an outline of the writing of chef Elizabeth David, who shared her skill with her readers by giving the cultural context of the food and its preparation. She writes about local cooks in France touching and prodding the bird. She tells stories about when, how and with whom she ate and gives interesting information about how tarragon might be used by Bordeaux cooks while, for the same recipe, sage was used by the cooks in Perpignan.

The fourth case study offered by Sennett is of Madame Benshaw and her recipe for *poulet à la d'Albufera*. Madame Benshaw is different from the others in that she talks almost entirely in something akin to riddles, devoid of instructions in the formal sense. Sennett was a student of hers at a night-school class, and he says that because her English was poor she would teach almost entirely by example, 'coupled with slight smiles and emphatic, frowning contradictions of her thick eyebrows'. With Sennett's help Madame Benshaw wrote down the recipe:

> Your dead child. Prepare him for new life. Fill him with the earth. Be careful! He should not over-eat. Put on his golden coat. You bathe him. Warm him but be careful! A child dies from too much sun. Put on his jewels. This is my recipe.

The 'dead child' meant the chicken. The 'preparation for new life' meant boning. 'Filling with earth' was about stuffing, and 'not over-eating' about not over-stuffing. The 'golden coat' was about browning before baking. The 'bathing' referred to preparation of a poaching liquor, and the 'jewels' the pouring on of this liquor.

The recipe is, then, told entirely through metaphors, and the metaphors allow the novice cook to feel and to understand: calling the chicken a 'child' immediately evokes a sense of intimacy, protection and tenderness, so readers understand that they should put the bird only in a cool oven. As Sennett puts it, metaphors 'roll forward and sideways' allowing the reader to garner different meanings as they do so.

Table 6.1   Styles of communication. A multiple case study

	Style (for comparison)	*Point being made*
Richard Olney	Straight instructions that give disinterested, clinical directions about what to do.	The general point is about learning coming from imagining and doing and using the knowledge learners already possess to help learn something new. It does not come through formal instruction.
Julia Child	Use of analogy; focus on the cook rather than the chicken; use of the learner's vulnerability.	
Elizabeth David	Talking about the culture; taking the reader on a journey; discussing variations in recipe – making it therefore less rigid, less fixed.	
Madame Benshaw	Talking entirely in metaphors that let the reader 'get inside' the mind of the chef and understand what she is saying.	

Through this comparative case study Sennett wants to make it clear that learning a craft is not about simply following instructions. The theoretical position that he evinces in the rest of his book is that learning is a human process, and in doing it we do well to follow our ready-made strengths – our 'instinct' for learning. His position is that learning happens by modelling and copying; by getting inside another person's head. He uses his comparative case study both to illustrate the theoretical position and to develop it.

Example 8: Acemoglu and Robinson – why nations fail

Acemoglu and Robinson (2012) ask at the outset of their book, *Why Nations Fail,* why some nations are more prosperous than others. They set out to provide evidence for a thesis that economic progress rests less on climate, geography or culture than it does on a nation's institutions. The success of a country's institutions rests, in turn, on the existence of fairness in the polity and the legislature. Only if these conditions are met can there be the possibility of economic expansion, wealth and peace.

They suggest that nations succeed because the people of successful countries 'overthrew the elites who controlled power and created a society where political rights were much more broadly distributed, where government was accountable and responsive to citizens, and where the great mass of people could take advantage of economic opportunities' (pp. 4–5). They had begun to espouse this theory elsewhere (e.g. Acemoglu et al., 2003) and it was very clearly the starting point of their work: it was a theory-first project to provide examples of the thesis which they had developed previously and which they were propounding. This presentation of an already formulated theoretical position stands as their **object**, to be illuminated and explicated by their case study. They provide a range of case studies, their **subjects**, across time and across continents to provide lenses through which to view the object – the theoretical position. The one we draw from here is 'The long agony of the Congo'.

The Congo (formerly, the Kingdom of Kongo), Acemoglu and Robinson argue from their reading of historical accounts, has over centuries been subject to 'extractive economic and political institutions'. It was the extractive nature of these institutions which gave rise to the reluctance of Kongolese farmers to adopt better technologies when they learned of them.

From the seventeenth century onwards, the Kingdom of Kongo was ruled hierarchically by a monarch and an elite of governors who controlled slave plantations and the collection of taxes across the country. The argument Acemoglu and Robinson make is that in order to make economic progress the ordinary citizenry would have needed to save and invest, but this was impossible given the arbitrary and punishing nature of taxation. Any extra production would have been expropriated by the elite. Rather than employ and benefit from new technology and infrastructure they would therefore shun it: they would, moreover, tend to move their habitations away from roads, for example, to reduce the possibility of plunder and to escape the reach of slave traders.

The Kongolese government provided few if any public services and no structure for governance such as secure property rights or law and order: 'On the contrary, the government was itself the biggest threat to its subjects' property and human rights' (2012: 90). Although the elite benefited from the Portuguese introduction of writing, there was no attempt to spread literacy to the population at large. During European colonization in the 19th century the imbalance of power became even more narrowly concentrated in a small elite. The modern Congo replicates the pattern: it illustrates 'the symbiotic relationship between political absolutism and economic institutions that empower and enrich a few at the expense of many' (ibid: 91). The political institutions of this country from the 17th century forwards contrast with those in countries where the power of an elite had been constrained and distributed more broadly.

One might argue that the presentation of this case does nothing to further our understanding since it outlines the facts but provides little in the way of analytical lever to the key issue in the phenomenon of development of economic prosperity, namely the factors which *enable* certain nation states to move toward inclusive political institutions and away from concentrations of power amongst an elite. Given that all elites try to preserve their power, what do citizenries have to do to enable them to escape from this?

Acemoglu and Robinson's case study is:

- a series of **key** cases, each illustrating and explicating a theoretical position;
- **instrumental**, since it serves a purpose;
- **illustrative**, since it is demonstrating the validity of an already-developed thesis; and
- **multiple/parallel**, since it is part of a series which demonstrate the thesis.

... and its methods are principally through documentary analysis.

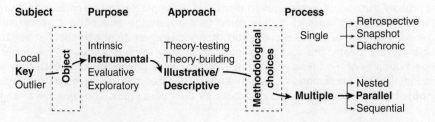

Figure 6.12 Acemoglu and Robinson's (2012) case study of failing nations

Example 9: Oliver Sacks – *An Anthropologist on Mars*

Although Oliver Sacks is a neurologist by professional training, he discards some of his neurological education to assume the clothes of a case inquirer. In doing this he talks with and observes people with certain kinds of behaviour stemming from syndromes such as autism and Tourette's – syndromes that lead people to display unusual and often disturbing behaviour. To do this, he follows these people through their lives in as straightforward a way as possible and comments on their everyday ways of living and ways of dealing with their behaviour in a social world that is often unsympathetic to difference.

In doing a set of case studies, Sacks offers a set of sparkling insights and understandings into the worlds of a number of people who behave differently. Such insights have been largely curtained off from us by the understanding offered by the traditional kinds of analysis found in medicine and psychology. As part of Sacks's discourse on our understanding of difference – of the 'borders of human experience', as he puts it – he quotes G.K. Chesterton:

> 'I don't deny the dry [scientific] light may sometimes do good, though in one sense it's the very reverse of science. So far from being knowledge, it's actually suppression of what we know. It's treating a friend as a stranger, and pretending that something familiar is really remote and mysterious.' (cited in Sacks, 1996: xvii)

Sacks gives reasons for eschewing many of the procedural and methodological habits of his own discipline, neurology. Neurologists focus on helping people who are, for whatever reason, uncomfortable, unhappy, disaffected, unable or unwilling to 'fit in'. Sacks's insight is that the methods which have been used to examine this discomfort or disaffection, while they can be successful up to a point, fail to address the real issues at stake, which are human issues. He says:

> The exploration of deeply altered selves and worlds is not one that can be fully made in a consulting room or office. The French neurologist François Lhemitte is especially sensitive to this, and instead of just observing his patients in the clinic, he makes a point of visiting them at home, taking them to restaurants or theatres, or for rides in this car, sharing their lives as much as possible. (It is similar, or was similar, with physicians in general practice. Thus when my father was reluctantly considering retirement at ninety, we said, 'At least drop the house calls.' But he answered, 'No, I'll keep the house calls – I'll drop everything else instead.') (Sacks, 1996: xvii–xviii)

Case study is like keeping the house calls. Sacks spent days and weeks with people with different kinds of behavioural issues – ones that caused them or those around them concerns of one kind or another. However, he made every effort to put those behaviours in context, not seeing them as disembodied, decontextualized medical or psychiatric conditions but rather as valid ways of dealing with the world, sometimes very successfully. For example, an autistic woman who found great difficulty relating with other people but who had great fondness and tenderness for animals combined the latter with her skill in drawing and planning. She used the latter to help her design slaughterhouses that minimized as far as possible any potential distress to the animals. Rather than defining a condition, or trying to exemplify or generalize from a condition with a supposedly typical example, Sacks used the intimate knowledge he was gathering to illustrate the idiosyncrasy, the particular story of this case. He showed the individual at work and at home. He showed her autonomy, her strength, her individuality and the integrity of her life. This is not something that could be said of most medical or psychological writing about autism.

Sacks makes no attempt to generalize from this or from any of his vignettes and his method is almost invisible, since he lays out no mental map at the beginning of his work. Rather, readers are left to make up their own minds: they are left to piece together conclusions for themselves. The conclusions – conclusions rather than generalizations – are about the ways in which difference can be respected rather than pigeon-holed. The pigeon-holing comes from the obvious categories of clinical and administrative convenience. And the emotions associated with those stereotypical categories lead too easily into hackneyed emotions of pity or admiration, so familiar to those with disabilities. By using the case study Sacks expects to move away from the categorical rut and offers us rich analyses of people's lives.

In terms of the taxonomy Sacks's work can be seen as in Figure 6.13.

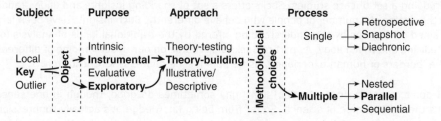

Figure 6.13 Sacks's (1996) work with people with different kinds of behavioural issues

a) The **subjects** of the study were the several people with whom he worked.
b) The **object** was to understand these people's worlds.
c) The subjects were **key** cases – in certain cases well-known – where the purpose was instrumental and exploratory and the approach was to develop an understanding about behaviour in context – as distinct perhaps from neurological dysfunction.
d) He went in to these situations with an open mind, hoping to **build theory** rather than test it.
e) The narrator and researcher used a wide range of **methods**, from observation to interview, but he principally used his own understanding of people. He used *himself.*
f) He used **multiple** cases, but these were not comparative in any significant way; rather, they were **parallel** to each other.

Example 10: Thomas, Walker and Webb – moving to inclusion

Thomas, Walker and Webb (1998) made a study of one school, which had been a special school for children and young people with physical disabilities and had converted itself into an *inclusion service*, providing an array of services and support to children attending local mainstream schools. The charity responsible for the school, Barnardo's, wanted to see how this had worked, from the development of the idea amongst the school's senior staff, to the dispersal of the school's students to local mainstream schools to the assimilation and inclusion of those students in their new schools. Although it would not be possible to generalize from this project to others, the evaluation of its progress and its achievements would undoubtedly provide lessons for ventures of a similar kind in the future.

The major focus in this evaluation was the experience of the young people themselves in their moves to both primary and secondary schools, but it was necessary also to see what the teachers and other staff were doing in their new teaching environments. The researchers needed to assess how teachers and assistants were helping class-teachers in differentiating the curriculum and modelling good practice. There needed to be an examination of how the new 'teacher-coordinators' worked with support services such as speech and language therapists and with parents – and an examination of how all these processes were managed in a time of flux.

With these varied foci, a broad-ranging case study was necessary. It needed to look in detail at what was happening to the teaching in the school, to parent involvement and to children's social adaptation. The researchers thus decided on a range of methods, from unstructured observation of what was happening in class to interviews with teachers, supporters and parents, to sociograms among the students.

The subject and the object of the study were closely linked and this piece of research was straightforwardly instrumental since the purpose of the study was evaluative. The object of the study concerned the extent to which this project had worked in the terms laid out by the school's managers at the outset, and the subject was the development and operation of the project. Any theoretical account that might 'thicken' around the object – about, for example, negotiation, involvement and participation – would be of value to other similar projects.

We can draw from two facets of the research actually undertaken and the methods used in its organization: at an interview with the headteacher and at an examination of one aspect of the social inclusion of the integrated children.

From the interview with the headteacher a personal account emerged of the changes in thinking which led the headteacher and his colleagues to embrace inclusion. This was not simply a technical description of change but a narrative about the way it happened – from the seed of an idea to the difficult and sometimes painful process of turning that idea to actuality. This included confronting the reality that a school which had been a second home to many children and a secure place of employment for staff would have to close. An extract from the interview (Thomas, Walker and Webb, 1998: 83–5) exemplifies this:

Interviewer: Could you tell me about how the inclusion initiative came about originally?

Headteacher: Yes. It's quite a long story really, I think, because there's two things that happened. If you like, there's the outer events and for me person-ally there were some inner things that were going on as well. In 1991, I'd been [headteacher] at the school three years, and in that time we increased the occupancy, we built the school up from a position where it had been in some difficulties, and it was doing well. So we agreed that at that point we would just look around and see what was on the horizon in special educational needs. And we looked at a lot of things, not just at inclusion. We looked at things like conductive education, special thera-pies, all sorts of stuff. One of the things that I went to, and Steve Connor went to, was the first Inclusion Conference, which was held in Cardiff ... Some of the things that George Flynn was saying about the outcomes for people who'd been in special education: joblessness, alcoholism, poten-tial for crime, vulnerability ... all those things hit me very powerfully at a time when I was personally feeling quite vulnerable. And also I think that the sense of – there was an alternative to the special school. And it affected me a lot ...

A host of matters was covered in the interview as a whole: the initial idea; the developing of a mission; the setting of working groups; the employment of consultants; the fears of staff, the anxieties of parents; the key role of the organizing charity as an institution which exists to promote children's interests; the role of the local authority and negotiations with them; the issue of choice for disabled people; the future.

What was striking from the interview was the way in which detailed plans arose not from some grand strategy and business plan. Instead, they grew out of the congruent personal philosophies of key staff, the chemistry of personal relationships and the happenstance of having local headteachers – and in particular one especially energetic and sympathetic head from a nearby primary school – who agreed with the special school headteacher and his colleagues and were prepared to take risks. It required a particular confluence of personalities and principles to make the project happen.

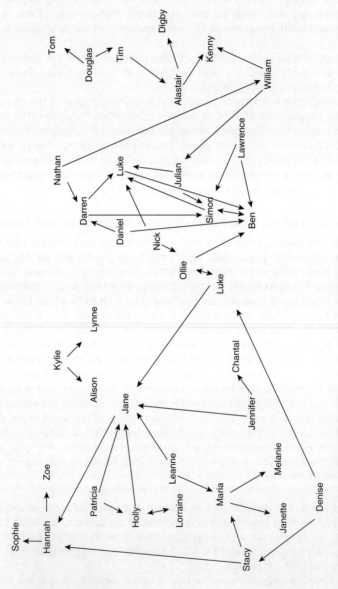

Figure 6.14 A sociogram of seating choices in a class with an included student

Another aspect of the research concerned the social inclusion of the children in class. As part of this, sociograms were used. Figure 6.14 shows one of these.

For the sociograms, the children of one class with an 'included' student were asked to say in confidence who they would like to sit next to or play with. The included student is Luke. It was interesting that in this class, and in each of the classes studied, an unremarkable pattern of relationships emerged for the included students. Even where the students had severe disabilities they emerged as well-integrated socially to their classes. For several of the 'included' children reciprocated choices were made. Interestingly, Luke is the only child crossing the gender barrier.

The various foci of the research – social, educational, organizational – all needed to be combined for a Gestalt, an overview, of the project and an assessment of the realization of its aims. The analysis which emerges from the combination of various kinds of research tells us a great deal about an undertaking of this kind – about preparation, negotiation and operation. All of the information has to be gathered and combined, in a process which links and interconnects ideas and insights.

Using the typology:

- this was a **single** study (since the project comprised one enterprise);
- it possessed linked **subject** and **object** and a variety of time use;
- it contained **retrospective, snapshot** and **diachronic** elements;
- it involved a **key** example of the process of change;
- it was done for **evaluation**;
- the aim was to examine the change and **build theory** about that change in particular, and also about change in general.

The trajectory through the typology is summarized in Figure 6.15.

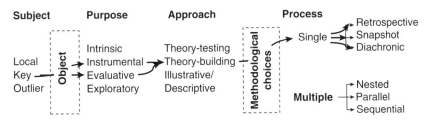

Figure 6.15 The study of the conversion of a school to an inclusion service

Conclusion

Running through the pieces in this chapter we can see varied kinds of selection, narrative and theorization; and there are varied uses of generalization and inference. However, in each piece of work reviewed it can be seen how the elements of a successful study are integrated via the form of the case study. In each case there is the careful, deliberate choice of a subject and a process to explicate and understand the object. In each there is judicious choice of methods and a conspicuous course of theory development. In each piece we can see how understanding is advanced using varied forms of the case study frame.

SEVEN

An example in depth:
Contesting certification

In this chapter we give an annotated case study with the intention of revealing in detail the 'anatomy' which we have been outlining in the book so far and in particular of throwing the spotlight on the process of theorization which is at the heart of the case study. The study, by one of the authors of this book (Myers, 2011), is of a working-class family in the 1930s which successfully resisted the pressure of the local authority to send the youngest child of the family to a residential special school. It raises a range of issues, from eugenics to the employment of psychometrics to the use of authority and professional power to the changing role of parents. It brings these together to provide a rich analysis of the ways in which forces interplay to develop, enact or resist policy. We annotate the study to indicate its anatomy and its route through the typology offered in Chapter 5.

That typology delineates a framework for thinking about and analyzing the structure of a case study, whether the researcher is conducting a study or reading it. The foundation stone for this structure involves an understanding of what the case study is for and what its elements achieve, with an emphasis on the subject–object distinction we drew earlier in this book. A key quotation from Wieviorka is worth repeating here:

> For a 'case' to exist, we must be able to identify a characteristic unit … This unit must be observed, but it has no meaning in itself. It is significant only if an observer … can refer it to an analytical category or theory. It does not suffice to observe a social phenomenon, historical event, or set of behaviors in order to declare them to be 'cases'. If you want to talk about a 'case', you also need the means of interpreting it or placing it in a context. (Wieviorka, 1992: 160)

As we discussed in Chapter 5, Wieviorka here makes it clear that there are two parts to the inquiry: (i) the analytical category, or theory, and (ii) the means for examining and illuminating that category. In stressing the separateness of the subject and the object in case study, Wieviorka highlights a distinction that is characteristic of all social inquiry. We discussed this distinction also in Chapter 5: the division that Wallace (1969: 3) drew between (i) the thing to be explained and (ii) the explanation itself in a piece of research. He called the former the *explanandum* and the latter the *explanans*. This is a distinction that marks all inquiry.

As a case study is conceived, conducted and written up it will take shape around the explanandum and explanans, which for the case study we have called the *object* and the *subject*. The object is the analytical lodestone for the research: it is what is to be explicated, the explanandum; it is the theory which is to be tested, built or developed. This testing, building or development happens via the narrative and the analysis of the subject, the explanans. The subject is, if you like, the lens through which the object is viewed, as indicated in Figure 7.1.

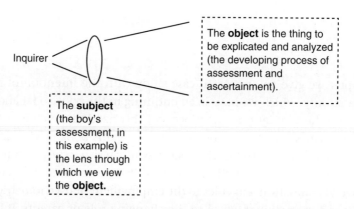

Inquirer

The **object** is the thing to be explicated and analyzed (the developing process of assessment and ascertainment).

The **subject** (the boy's assessment, in this example) is the lens through which we view the **object.**

Figure 7.1 Viewing the object for analysis via the subject of the case study

In this case study, the object – the theme on which the author intends to throw light – is the process by which children were (and still are, in much assessment) ascertained as being mentally deficient. This is a process that developed out of the growth of psychometrics early in the 20th century and out of a pre-Second World War conviction in a certain kind of social Darwinism – a confidence in the notion that for the sustenance of the national gene pool, those with disabilities (and even those who were less able) had to be segregated away from the mainstream of society. As many commentators have pointed out, the way in which policy develops out of such beliefs happens through a swirl of politics and fashionable ideas – not through an objective, neutral course of disinterested policy development. What Foucault, for example, reveals in his historical studies on sexuality, madness, medicine and prisons are the ways in which ideas and practices are taken up and become more or less unquestioned elements of received knowledge and the practice of professionals, institutions and authorities – how they become part of the 'political economy of power'. Foucault suggests that policy develops out of 'a multiplicity of often minor processes of different origin, of scattered location which overlap' (Foucault, 1991: 138).

The study examines the way in which ideas such as this are translated into practice through certain kinds of supposedly scientific technology (such as psychometric tests) which are used both to ascertain putative deficits and then in turn are used to legitimate institutionalization. But it also questions at the outset the extent to which Foucault's *power* is at the core of this process, indicating that recent cultural histories suggest that the processes involved are characterized more by 'compromises between a psychology (or more properly, psychologies) struggling for survival amongst established patterns and idioms of British cultural life'. The process, if it can be called that, is more random and messy than a Foucauldian analysis might indicate.

The author of this case study, Myers, aims to shine light on this process – on the process by which ideas turn into policy – illuminating its lineaments and interstices via case study. He does this through a close examination of the subject of the study – the Keasley family and the various players who were involved in the ascertainment of one of the family's children, Stanley, who was described as 'slow' at school. It outlines the background of one of the principal actors in the *dramatis personae* of the tale, Dr Boycott, and the scientistic intellectual hinterland in which Boycott must have developed his ideas about mental capacity and educability.

In the annotation of the case study that follows, we show how the object is contextualized via its situation in the background to the topic of the work. The background, as given in the introduction to the report, outlines the common ground concerning the topic; it is the context within which the work is situated. The object emerges from some issue or 'angle' within that context – some missing evidence, some absence of analysis or some dilemma in the existing literature. Following this, there is an account of how the research addresses that absence or dilemma – an account of the promise of elucidation.

A research report will also contain outlines of the methods used in the study. There will follow the narrative itself, the account of the subject's circumstances and story, with theorization, analysis and synthesis as the account proceeds. These are all noted in our commentary.

The report of this case study thus contains different elements:

- The **background** to the topic.
- The **issue** which emerges from that background – the object (or explanandum, or analytical core to be explicated).
- An account of the **subject** – the person, event, phenomenon which is being used as a lens through which to view the object (the explanans).
- Outlines, as appropriate, of the **methodology** employed – of how data are being accessed and collected.
- A **narrative** – the telling of a story about the events running alongside the subject of the study.

- **Analysis** and synthesis – the connection of the findings to the analytical frame of the study: the connection, in other words, of the subject to the object.
- **Theorization**, as the report of the study progresses, involving the analysis which is being undertaken, especially insofar as this relates to previous work on the subject as noted in the literature.

We give in the following annotation an edited version of the published case study, with the commentary according to these bullet points alongside the original text.

Contesting certification: mental deficiency, families and the State in interwar England

Abstract

This article is an attempt to shed some further light on the people and the processes involved in the identification of mental deficiency in children and young people. In order to do this it turns away from the themes that have been most prominent in the historiography to date: elite and professional ideas, parliamentary and public debates and the formulation of policy. Instead the paper is concerned with a single instance of diagnosis of imbecility in an 11 year old schoolboy in a rural village in the English county of Hertfordshire. As far as is possible it reconstructs this diagnosis and charts and explains a remarkable and successful challenge to it in the High Court. In doing so it draws on a variety of documentary records – educational, legal and medical – as well as the testimony of some of the surviving members of the family concerned. In employing these sources particular attention is paid to the actions of the people involved in diagnosis, and it seeks to explain and understand those actions with explanatory tools taken from cultural history.

Introduction

Recently a number of studies have been published which focus on the influence of psychological thought and practice around the world. In this work psychological thought is emerging as a much more diverse and protean field than was previously recognized; popular as well as professional, mystical as much as rational, often individualized and introspective, but also championed as a progressive human science with the potential to effect social transformation through educational schemes of self-improvement and elite programmes of social administration.[1]

Commentary

Abstract, which includes:
Statement of the analytical frame, or object.
Statement of the subject of the case study.
Statement of the methods used.
Statement of the purpose in further understanding of the object.

Background: The nature and influence of psychological thought and how it has grown and changed.

---

[1]Ellie Zaretsky (2004) *Secrets of the Soul: A Social and Cultural History of Psychoanalysis.* New York: Knopf.

This is an important historiographical advance. It alerts historians and educationalists to the existence of a rich psychological culture in which new – or at least significantly modified – ways of understanding human character or identity emerged. These diverse ideas were, of course, controversial and they were variously applied, frustrated and spurned in complex ways across different social, institutional and discursive sites.

In England one such site has been education. In an important challenge to much recent work that has emerged from a distinctively cultural history of education, Mathew Thomson points towards the limitations of studies inspired by Michel Foucault. Rejecting the predominant themes of control and regulation, Thomson explores a messy series of compromises between a psychology (or more properly, psychologies) struggling for survival amongst established patterns and idioms of British cultural life.[2] Child guidance clinics, for example, were few in number and badly resourced because of the established dislike of taxation. Behaviourism had limited appeal because it sat uneasily with existing discourses of character and self-improvement. Similarly, mental testing was sporadic and inconsistent partly because the assumption that intelligence was fixed was unpopular with the self-improving ethos of the period, and partly because teachers were ill-informed and unenthusiastic about them.[3]

Background: Psychology is at odds with everyday thought. Relationship to existing literature, pointing out the tension between a Foucauldian analysis and one which pointed to a more arbitrary and haphazard process of policy development. This is the beginning of the issue to be explicated.

In many respects this picture of psychology mirrors recent developments in the study of psychiatry.[4] Here, Thomson's related and important work on psychiatry, eugenics and mental deficiency similarly challenged a historiography permeated by notions of control and regimentation and emphasized that although an emerging psychiatric profession – and the voluntary agencies with which it worked – was influential in the development of institutional solutions, that influence was challenged and constrained by a variety of political, social and administrative factors.

Background: The standard picture is that psychiatry, like psychology, sought institutional solutions to issues such as 'mental deficiency'. But there were competing social and intellectual currents. The 'standard picture' is therefore challenged.

---

[2]Mathew Thomson (2006) *Psychological Subjects: Identity, Culture and Health in Twentieth-Century Britain*. Oxford: Oxford University Press, pp. 6–8.

[3]Thomson (2006) *Psychological Subjects: Identity, Culture and Health in Twentieth-Century Britain*. Oxford: Oxford University Press, Chapter 4.

[4]Marijke Gijswijt-Hofstra and Roy Porter (eds) (1998) *Cultures of Psychiatry and Mental Health Care in Postwar Britain and the Netherlands*. Amsterdam: Wellcome. Mathew Thomson (1995) 'Mental hygiene as an international movement', in Paul Weindling (ed.), *International Health Organisations and Movements*. Cambridge: Cambridge University Press.

So whilst eugenic psychiatrists might have championed institutional solutions to the perceived problem of mental deficiency, these were constrained by strong humanitarian and libertarian strands in politics, by the commitment to notions of educability in the school system, by the social stigma attached to incarceration and by the mundane but very important complexities of administering and delivering policy on the ground.[5] In short, Thomson has made important and groundbreaking contributions to the history of both psychological and psychiatric thought and practice in England. Yet in two key areas, one empirical and one conceptual, there is room for further discussion and analysis.

Thomson's *Problem of Mental Deficiency* remains the best available account of the complex and controversial processes involved in identifying the mentally and socially deficient in British history. However, and despite the case studies included at the end of the book, relatively little is known about either the people who were the target of these policies or those who enacted them. This is a significant absence. After all, a good deal of social and cultural history remains committed to a project of historical recovery in the hope that it will foster positive individual and collective identities. This is one of the reasons why the inclusion in historical narratives of individuals and groups affected by the growing power of medical surveillance is so important.[6] Yet there are empirical as well as ethical reasons for wanting to say more about those who were the target of the psychology, psychiatry and psychoanalysis. The interwar period is now portrayed by historians as an era in which an increasingly popular psychology of potential developed alongside the growing influence of an idealized and affectionate nuclear family. In such families fathers were, rhetorically and perhaps actually, increasingly home and child-centred with a recognized, if rather constrained role to play, in helping children realize that potential.

Background: Who identifies 'mental deficiency'?

Issue: The missing evidence/analysis is identified.
Need for this to be a case study – to get direct first-hand source material.

Issue: Place of the family – neglected from much analysis.

Issue: The missing evidence/analysis is identified.

---

[5]Mathew Thomson (1998) *The Problem of Mental Deficiency. Eugenics, Democracy and Social Policy in Britain, c.1870–1939*. Oxford: Clarendon.

[6]Steve Humphries and P. Gordon (1992) *Out of Sight: The Experience of Disability 1900–1950*. Plymouth: Northcote House. Dorothy Atkinson, Mark Jackson and Jan Walmsley (eds) (1997) *Forgotten Lives: Exploring the History of Learning Disability*. Kidderminster: British Institute of Learning Disabilities.

In these circumstances psychiatric diagnosis and the punitive measures that could follow were potentially divisive and so, logically at least, extremely contentious. Yet, as Peter Bartlett has argued, 'the nuts and bolts questions of how doctors and other social administrators determined whether an individual fell into the class of the feeble-minded (or mentally deficient)' largely remain unanswered.[7] Little is known about who practically identified mentally deficient people and there has been a paucity of work exploring how such decisions were communicated, administered and received.

This article is an attempt to shed some further light on the people and the processes involved in the identification of mental deficiency in children and young people. In order to do this it turns away from the themes that have been most prominent in the historiography to date: elite and professional ideas, parliamentary and public debates and the formulation of policy. Instead the paper is concerned with a single instance of diagnosis of imbecility in an 11 year old schoolboy in a rural village in the English county of Hertfordshire. As far as is possible it reconstructs this diagnosis and charts a remarkable and successful challenge to it in the High Court. In doing so it draws on a variety of documentary records – educational, legal and medical – as well as the testimony of some of the surviving members of the family concerned.

Issue: The central issue is summarized – about who identifies mental deficiency, and the need to do this, given the somewhat detached analysis in the literature until now.

In employing these sources particular attention is paid to the actions of the people involved in diagnosis, and it seeks to explain and understand those actions with explanatory tools taken from cultural history. The turn to cultural history can be partly explained by the switch from the micro to the macro: it helps explain the significance of what otherwise might be considered parochial or antiquarian. However, the turn to cultural history has hardly been without controversy. This much is clear from reviews of Mathew Thomson's work where his choice of explanatory framework and his interrogation of new sources has been praised by historians and often interpreted as constituting a rejection of 'disciplinary history'.[8]

Explanation of how the case will address the issue – how, in other words, the subject will elucidate the object and how this elucidation will contribute to understanding of the object.

---

[7] Peter Bartlett (2006) 'Reviews in History 289: Review of Mark Jackson: Borderland of Imbecility', Institute of Historical Research. Available at: www.history.ac.uk/reviews (accessed 23 October 2006).

[8] Alison Falby, Peter Barham and Graham Richards (2007) 'Reviews of psychological subjects', *History of the Human Sciences*, 20(3): 123–9.

Adrian Wooldridge's history of educational psychology, for example, is largely biographical. Any interest in the structural factors that might have underpinned the emergence of educational psychology, such as relationships of class, gender and race; disability; a newly interventionist state; a slow shift to democracy; a populist demand for welfare capitalism, are dismissed as 'polemical' or 'neo-Marxist' and there is a flat refusal of the idea that knowledge has social origins. The result is a liberal history of progress in which a new science slowly disperses ignorance and superstition and shines new light on children and their learning.[9] Or, to take a more nuanced example, Thomson argues that demands for welfare support and institutions of care for the feeble-minded are evidence of the fact that new legislation and institutions for the mentally defective cannot 'exclusively be attributed to the imposition of a more prescriptive view of normality'.[10] Family demands for welfare support and care are interpreted as evidence of the fact that psychological thought was not imposed from above in a straightforwardly repressive and constraining manner. Instead, it is important to retain a view of power as productive and to remember that projects of governance may generate subjectivities, or forms of self dependent on other social actors and other knowledge. In this view, demands for legislation and institutions may not be simple expressions of freedom but a sign of the success of the moral regulation projects that sought to create the ideal citizens for a market economy. This, of course, is a matter for debate. The simple point here is that both the rise of psychology and the exercise of highly constrained choice are best understood against a proper explanation and analysis of relevant social structures. Perhaps the point being laboured here – the need to steer a course between excessively empirical studies, where structure is a suspicious idea, and a strong constructionism in which meaningful action disappears – is best illustrated in the course of the article. This consists of three parts.

Issue: Knowledge has social origins but this is unacknowledged in the history of educational psychology.

Explanation of why case study – why this form of inquiry – is appropriate in these circumstances.

---

[9]Adrian Wooldridge (1994) *Measuring the Mind: Education and Psychology in England, c.1860–1990.* Cambridge: Cambridge University Press, pp. 2, 6–10. For a contrasting and provocative interpretation reached by way of a sociology of knowledge see John White (2006) *Intelligence, Destiny and Education: The Ideological Roots of Intelligence Testing.* London: Routledge.

[10]Mathew Thomson (2001) 'Psychology and the "Consciousness of Modernity" in Early Twentieth-Century Britain', in Martin Daunton and Bernhard Rieger (eds), *Meanings of Modernity: Britain from the Late Victorian Era to World War II.* Oxford: Berg, p. 108.

The first part of the article relates a brief history of the Keasley family and the examination of their son, Stanley, in 1937.

Outline of the subject of the case study through which the object is being viewed.

In doing so it presents a conventional historical narrative that seeks to historicize the actors and the processes involved in Stanley's diagnosis. In other words, it situates this particular story within wider and well-known social forces; the development of a regulatory state, the political concern with families and their children, the empowering of professionals to enact this concern, and the relationships of class that permeated that professional discourse.

An account of how the research addresses the issues at the heart of the topic.

Much of this narrative is reconstructed using conventional historical sources – local health and education records, political debates and so on – but it also draws on an oral history interview conducted with some surviving family members. This interview was recorded with two sisters of now deceased Stanley and, as with disability history more generally, it plays an important evidential role in what follows.[11] The interview not only helped to augment the documents in the archive, it also allowed a silenced family narrative to emerge that helps us to understand the processes at work and their significance. Ethically it is important to recognize that this is, therefore, in one sense a shared narrative. An important element of what follows emerges from that interview and subsequent correspondence with the author that clarified issues and discussed an earlier draft of this article.[12]

An outline of certain of the methods being employed in studying the subject and why these are felt to be appropriate.

The second section of the article focuses on families and subjectivities to narrate the reaction of Stanley's family to his diagnosis and seeks to account for their remarkable legal challenge. In doing so the article moves towards more cultural territory; it considers changing forms of subjectivity for parents or, more specifically, fathers in the interwar period. It tentatively suggests that fatherhood, and the changing forms of emotional and affective life apparent in that role, may be important in explaining processes of classification and reactions to them. A third and final section offers some observations on the wider significance of this story.

Outline of the forthcoming analysis – the connection between the case (subject) and a certain aspect of the analytical frame (object). This is an account of how the research addresses that missing evidence or dilemma – an account of the promise of elucidation.

[11]Karen Hirsch (1998) 'Culture and Disability: The Role of Oral History', in Robert Perks and Alistair Thomson (eds) *The Oral History Reader*. London: Routledge.

[12]Sheena Rolph and Jan Walmsley (2006) 'Oral history and new orthodoxies: narrative accounts in the history of learning disability', *Oral history*, 34(1): 81–91.

A family under examination[13]

Stanley Keasley was born into the small village of Harpenden in Hertfordshire on 3 May 1927. His father, Russell, was born in 1894 (and died in 1971) and was brought up in the East End of London. He served in the 1914–1918 war where he sustained a bullet wound. Stanley's mother was born in 1897 in the rather different environment of rural Bendish (near Hitchin) where she worked, like so many other women in the region, as a basket weaver. These environments, so different from each other geographically and culturally, were bridged by a Sunday bicycle ride that started a romance that ended in marriage in 1920. Three sons were born to the couple over the next seven years: in 1921, 1924 and Stanley in 1927. The young family settled in Harpenden sometime around Stanley's birth and local trade directories suggest his family moved three times in the next ten years, a journey that took the Keasley family from a rented terraced house to purchasing a bungalow with a small-holding attached to it with the help of a loan from the Co-operative Society.[14]

An account of the subject of the case study.

For most of this period Stanley's father worked in printing as a machine setter for the Amalgamated Press. He worked on the night shift and made the 30 mile journey to London by bus or train in the early evening and returned home early next morning. At other times, and for reasons that are not entirely clear, he took breaks from printing and took work that was closer to home; a period as a milkman is one clear memory of his daughters. What may be significant about this pattern of employment is that this was a father who was, to a considerable degree, present in the house and in the daily routines of family life.

The subject of the case study (continued). Attention is drawn to a particular feature of this case study, namely the involvement of the father in the home and the family.

Stanley started attending the local elementary school in September 1932 and appears to have been in regular and unremarkable attendance until 1937. His sisters remember his scholarly progress as 'slow' and as confirming the family knowledge that Stanley found formal academic learning difficult. Additional lessons provided by family friends to help progress his reading and writing yielded no marked improvement, and his speech was remembered as difficult to understand.

The subject of the case study (continued).
The point is being made that although Stanley is a little slow at school, he seems to have no difficulties outside school.

---

[13]This section draws on the author's interview with Marie Clarke and Peggy Gageley, Harpenden, 25 January 2008. Transcript and correspondence in author's possession.

[14]*Kelly's Trade Directory of St. Alban's, Harpenden and Hatfield 1938–39.*

An operation to remove Stanley's adenoids around 1934 or 1935 brought no marked changes. He transferred to the senior department of his elementary school in September 1935. Yet despite evident difficulties with academic progress, Stanley's sisters do not remember any complaints about his behaviour at school, or any difficulties in his relationships with pupils or teachers. There is no extant documentary evidence that testifies to such problems. Outside school hours Stanley was often with his father, spending long hours tending to the pigs and chickens kept on the family small-holding. In fact, the motivation for moving to this property may have been the desire of Stanley's parents to do what they thought was best for him. Although it had smaller living accommodation, the land that accompanied it allowed Stanley to practise work about which he was both enthusiastic and competent.

Even though there is an obvious danger of inventing an idealized and idyllic picture of childhood, it does seem as though Stanley, sometimes working late into the night at a hobby he was enthused by, often with his father, protected by a loving family and well-known in the local community, was a happy and loving child.

The subject of the case study. As above, the particular features of this study are made clear: it is a close and loving family – perhaps unusually close and loving, with particular consequences for the course of the story.

Stanley underwent a medical examination in 1937, two years after his transfer to the senior department of his local elementary school. That examination was conducted by Dr Arthur Norman Boycott who had graduated Doctor of Medicine from the University of London in 1893. The date may be considered significant both because it saw the foundation of the Darwinian inspired Child Study Movement in the UK, and because it was the year in which psychiatry instruction, but not examination, became a compulsory part of undergraduate medical examination.[15] Boycott's formal education in his future specialism was therefore likely to be framed in a rather general biological and heredity framework but limited insofar as specialist study was concerned; it perhaps amounted to no more than an independent engagement with the growing number of psychiatry textbooks designed for students. Yet these textbooks, and individuals like Boycott who might have read them, were certainly decisive in what Nikolas Rose has called the construction of modern selves.

The central character of the case study (Stanley) meets another key character (Dr Boycott), whose background as a doctor is outlined.

Boycott's acquisition of a biological frame of reference for understanding 'backwardness' at school married with the rise of psychological assessment and ideas of 'regulation' by the state.

---

[15]William F. Bynum (1991) 'Tuke's Dictionary and Psychiatry at the Turn of the Century', in German E. Berrios and Hugh Freeman (eds) *150 Years of British Psychiatry, 1841–1991*. London: Gaskell, pp. 169, 176.

Briefly, between 1870 and 1925 the rise of the psy disciplines, 'their languages, types of explanation and judgement, their techniques and their expertise', began to influence the ways in which people thought about and imagined their own subjectivity.[16] Thomson has similarly argued that although there were limitations to the application of these ideas, the outstanding development of the era was the 'regulation of the psychological subject from above'. Ordinary people 'inhabited a world in which their consciousness was beginning to be measured, classified and managed with direct consequences for their life opportunities whether they knew about it or not'.[17] Boycott was amongst the first generation of those proliferating experts whose activities were central to the expansion of the state. They were crucial in the identification of 'problem' groups and behaviours, and the strategies they helped to devise in order to cure or contain them slowly became more invasive.

Strategies for the cure and containment of problem groups and behaviours obviously required experts who, in turn, benefitted from the increasing availability of professional opportunities. Yet, quite how these opportunities were experienced in practice remains under researched. Published research on the school medical service in Britain has tended to concentrate on macro questions of finance, policy and administration.[18] And even where medical officers do appear in historical narratives there is a tendency to read off their identities and attitudes from the monographs, annual reports and submissions to official investigations produced by elite actors. By way of contrast, Louise Westwood's recent study provides interesting evidence of how women were not just victims of psychiatry, but also beneficiaries of the roles that it opened up, even if these often remained outside the institutional mainstream.[19]

Boycott is a key actor in the dramatis personae, playing a central role in explaining the course of events. His place in the school medical service is outlined. The significance of the school medical service is explained.

His background as a doctor in the 'great confinement' of the 'mentally ill' is outlined.

[16]Nikolas Rose (1997) 'Assembling the Modern Self', in Roy Porter (ed.), *Rewriting the Self: Histories from the Renaissance to the Present*. London: Routledge, pp. 224–48.

[17]Mathew Thomson (2001) 'Psychology and the "Consciousness of Modernity" in Early Twentieth-Century Britain', in Martin Daunton and Bernhard Rieger (eds), *Meanings of Modernity: Britain from the Late Victorian Era to World War II*. Oxford: Berg, pp.107–08.

[18]Bernard Harris (1995) *The Health of the Schoolchild: A History of the School Medical Service in England and Wales*. Buckingham: Open University Press.

[19]Louise Westwood (2006) 'Separatism and Exclusion: Women in Psychiatry from 1900–1960', in Pamela Dale and Joseph Melling (eds), *Mental Illness and Learning Disability Since 1850: Finding a Place for Mental Disorder in England*. London: Routledge.

However, the general paucity of biographical and prosopographical studies of these new experts (particularly in the field of education) means that it is difficult to assess the typicality of Norman Boycott's career. His first professional appointment, testimony to the great confinement of the late 19th century, was almost certainly at the Surrey County Asylum, Cane Hill, near Coulsdon. He was appointed Superintendent at the Hertfordshire County Asylum (or Hill End) in 1898, arriving in December, some four months before its official opening and whilst construction was still ongoing. Initially designed to accommodate some 800 patients, Hill End was designed by the influential and prolific G.T. Hine who carved out a successful career as a specialist in the field of asylum buildings. Engaged on an initial salary of £500 per annum, Boycott's duties were many and varied in this early period. He engaged all the people employed at the asylum, invited tenders for the supply of shrubs, made recommendations for salary increases, submitted lists of required appliances for the farm and dairy and furnished his own cottage on asylum grounds with institutional funds.[20] Boycott moved into the superintendent's cottage in December 1900 and from there presided over the expansion of the asylum and its facilities, and all its activities, for the next 25 years. There were physical changes to the building: a dark room was added in 1901 and a bigger photographic room followed in 1905; two new admission blocks, one for men and one for women, were approved in 1914. There were also occasional innovations in daily routines: Boycott introduced an annual ball for staff and purchased pianos for use in wards. Most of all, however, Boycott spent some 27 years performing the established rituals of asylum practice: he admitted patients, examined expanding registers, walked the corridors and toured the wards of this vast building.

Thousands of patients passed through Hill End Asylum during Boycott's long years as superintendent. Every diagnosis he made and medical decision he took were, in one sense, an exercise of power. Anderson, the author of an unpublished history of the Hill End Hospital offers a picture of the young Boycott as an idealistic humanitarian. Boycott wants to cure his patients, or at least make them sufficiently well to allow discharge.

The case begins to be explicated as we start to understand how a professional's determination to accumulate power and status via his success in 'curing' patients has consequences in the shape and provision of services.

---

[20]Hertfordshire Record Office (HRO), Hertfordshire County Lunatic Asylum, Abstracts of Minutes, 27 February 1900–25 March 1903.

Yet early in his career he is already complaining that he is receiving the wrong category of patient: most were judged by him to be chronically ill and to have little chance of recovery. In his report for the year ending 31 March 1901, Boycott estimated that of the 333 patients then at Hill End only four could be considered as having a chance of recovery. This, he complained, was a misuse of resources with damaging effects to the asylum community:

'It is good for morale of both staff and patients when new cases come in and get well. At present we have a new asylum, with modern appliances being used simply as a storehouse for chronic and irrecoverable patients.'[21]

Use of evidence: A direct quotation from Boycott.

Whether Boycott's own morale, and his optimistic view of at least some forms of mental illness, survived the many years of growing patient numbers who were rarely cured must be open to doubt. Anderson certainly suggests that Boycott quickly became a frustrated and disillusioned medic. Working in a field lacking in status and esteem, in charge of a storehouse for chronic patients with little hope of recovery, Boycott's time would most likely have been spent with the administrative procedures that were such a characteristic part of psychiatric medicine.[22]

Theorization on the professional's motivation.

Boycott's retirement did not, however, mean the end of his career. In an example of the ways in which psychiatrists and psychiatric perspectives could be influential beyond the confines of institutional spaces and disciplinary specialism, Boycott soon took on a peripatetic post with the school medical service examining, visiting and reporting on cases under the 1913 Mental Deficiency Act and the 1914 Elementary Education (Defective and Epileptic Children) Act. Under the former legislation, the local state had a duty to ascertain, certify and make provision for mental defectives in their areas and such provision was envisaged as encompassing institutional care, a system of guardianship or statutory and voluntary supervision in the community. Under the latter legislation a separate system of education and care was established for all children under the age of 17.

Theorization on the professional's motivation, and its consequences in the construction of the special school system ... and one in particular: Kingsmead.

[21]HRO, Off. Acc. 1025: B. Anderson (n.d.) *History of Hill End Hospital*, pp. 15.

[22]HRO, Off. Acc. 1025: B. Anderson (n.d.), *Hill End Hospital*, pp. 170–71. On the status of psychiatry see Mathew Thomson (1998) *The Problem of Mental Deficiency. Eugenics, Democracy and Social Policy in Britain*, c.1870–1939. Oxford: Clarendon, pp. 120–21.

In Boycott's place of peripatetic employment the duty of care had been met by the opening of a new residential special school, Kingsmead, for 150 'educable and improvable mentally defective children' in 1919.[23]

David Parker attributes the opening of this special school, and the administration of the system for mental defectives, to the influence of the school medical officer between 1919 and 1940, Dr Henry Hyslop Thomson.[24] Thomson had significant influence in local government. He championed welfare reforms during and after World War I and, argues Parker, 'aspects of special education became Thomson's jealously guarded personal preserve'.[25] Thomson's missionary zeal was required early in the life of Kingsmead when the parents of 37 of the first 50 children recommended for transfer refused their children's admission. This level of opposition was probably not a surprise. The debates over the 1914 Education Act in both Houses of Parliament had continually returned to the principles and the practices of identifying mentally deficient children and sending them away from families for residential care. Despite lengthy debate, and a particular libertarian concern about the growing intrusion of the state into family life that can also have been seen elsewhere in continental Europe and North America, it was both the intention and the effect of the legislation that this decision be transferred to representatives of the State. For if, in theory, the state upheld the privacy of the family by making transfer to special schooling conditional on the written consent of the parents, it qualified this consent by stating that it could not be 'unreasonably withheld'.[26] Ultimately, and in practice, judgements about sound reasoning were in the hands of medical and other lay professionals.[27]

Theorization: professional power and its part in determining how ascertainment should take place. Doctors were developing and defending this role.

---

[23]David Parker (1998)'"A convenient dispensary": elementary education and the influence of the school medical service 1907–39', *History of Education*, 27(1): 77.

[24]Parker (1998) 'A convenient dispensary' (see above); Henry Hyslop Thomson, Medical Doctor (Glasgow) 1898. Died 1950. See obituary in *British Medical Journal*, 27 May 1950, p. 1274.

[25]Parker (1998) 'A convenient dispensary' (see above), p. 77.

[26]1914 Elementary Education (Defective and Epileptic Children) Act, s.2.

[27]Pamela Dale (2006) 'Tension in the voluntary-statutory alliance: "lay professionals" and the planning and delivery of mental deficiency services, 1917–45', in Pamela Dale and Joseph Melling (eds) *Mental Illness and Learning Disability Since 1850: Finding a Place for Mental Disorder in England*. London: Routledge, pp. 154–78.

In parliamentary debates the President of the Board of Education, Joseph Pease, defended the expertise of medical practitioners employed by the Board of Education and was at pains to defend the jurisdiction of the doctor over the identification of the mentally deficient child: 'though I agree that those who have had teaching experience of these children ought to be consulted, after all the evidence has been secured, I think the final decision must be with a medical man'.[28] That decision was formalized in the requirement that two medical signatures were required to confirm a child's mental deficiency and, despite arguments for a diagnostic role for a teacher, their relegation to an advisory capacity. Medicine, in the shape of School Medical Officers and their staff, were given the authority to judge the present state and future potential of the child. In doing so the state and the law sought from medicine expertise as to the psychology of the child: it was, publicly at least, a definitive science charged with establishing the medical facts of particular cases.

Theorization on the construction of medical status and influence.

Despite the anticipated and actual opposition to the transfer of children to special schools, Thomson persisted in Hertfordshire. His tendency, notes Parker, was to equate 'parental intransigence with ingratitude' and he was more than prepared to resort to legal compulsion the moment persuasion had failed'.[29] This was a determination born partly from the long-established ambivalence that physicians displayed in their attitudes to the parents of children they assessed, but strengthened by the growing conviction in the interwar period that parental ignorance and neglect were the root causes of mental deficiency.[30] Residential schooling was the source of hope because it could offer intensive training removed from the baleful effects of parents and Thomson continued to push for early diagnosis and transfer, despite the evident controversies that it caused. In 1925, for example, he persuaded the education committee to purchase an intelligence test to encourage the identification of children who would benefit from special schooling.

Theorization on the power of medics in the developing process of ascertainment and their confidence in the legitimacy of the process vis-à-vis the views of parents.

Psychological assessment is used as a 'scientific' tool in legitimizing the process of ascertainment and special education.

---

[28]*House of Commons Debates*, 5 May 1914, vol. 62, cc166–227.

[29]David Parker (1998) '"A convenient dispensary": elementary education and the influence of the school medical service 1907–39', *History of Education*, 27(1): 77.

[30]Jonathan Gillis (2005) 'Taking a medical history in childhood illness: representations of parents in pediatric texts since 1850', *Bulletin of the History of Medicine*, 79: 400, 412–15.

Parker argues that he was one of those medical progressives driven by the idea that accurate diagnosis would facilitate specific systems of education that would ultimately bring improved learning. Responsible for the assessment and classification of children, the role of the school medical officer, and the kinds of ideas and frameworks that they drew on and applied were quite clearly crucial.

Mark Jackson is one of a number of authors who have argued that the medical section at the Board of Education, and school medical officers more generally, did not share the eugenic or hereditarian views that prevailed in other departments of government or wider civil society. Far from insisting on a biological explanation for mental deficiency, these officials worked to promote the notion of educability and attempted to delay classification so that every child had a good chance of displaying their capacity for learning (however this was defined).[31] A similarly positive view of other professionals employed in the education system is apparent in other work. Mathew Thomson, for example, argues that teachers showed little support for abstract mental testing but were enthusiastic about a child-centred psychology that could promote new and meaningful forms of learning.[32] Similarly, Sutherland argues that where testing was adopted, it was characterized by a complex view of intelligence and a sophisticated attempt to balance some of the weaknesses of the tests.[33] These arguments, and the implicit professionalization narratives in which knowledge and empathy incrementally develop, are best treated with caution. Arguably the definitive statement of interwar school medical practice, James Kerr's weighty *Fundamentals of School Health*, finished a long chapter on 'subnormal intelligence' that reviewed evidence from North America and continental Europe by reminding his readers of their public duty as scientific professionals:

'Allowing for wastage from migration and death, two-thirds of the mental defectives should have constant custodial treatment from school days on,

Theorization: There are others in the system who reject the thinking behind medical assessment of 'subnormal intelligence'.

However, the dominant view was biological and eugenic.

Use of evidence: Direct quotation from the time.

---

[31]Mark Jackson (2000) *The Borderland of Imbecility: Medicine, Society and the Fabrication of the Feeble Mind in Late Victorian England*. Manchester: Manchester University Press, pp. 110–11, 251.

[32]Matthew Thomson (2006) *Psychological Subjects: Identity, Culture, and Health in Twentieth-Century Britain*. Oxford: Oxford University Press. pp. 126–32.

[33]Gillian Sutherland (1984) *Ability, Merit and Measurement*. Oxford: Oxford University Press.

not merely as a matter of State economy, but so that by direction and regulation of their activities they may make the fullest and happiest use of their lives, the common aim of all. As concerns the community they are nothing but a burden which is constantly increasing, so that now it has become a public duty to prevent these people coming into existence, so far as that is possible. This is a purely scientific question, and will only benefit coming generations, but it is a duty with which no idle speculative sentiments or vain religious scruples should be permitted to interfere and for their own happiness, as well as the benefit of others, they should be sterilized'.[34]

Judging by this advice, it might be supposed that many policy-makers, doctors and teachers still supported the idea that the classification of children on the basis of different and relatively fixed levels of mental capacity was both possible and desirable. In this respect the rather ambivalent attitude of educationalists to psychological testing can be misleading. Whilst teachers cautioned against the exclusive use of tests for classification, and argued that their experience was a necessary part of knowing the child, they did not fundamentally depart from the view that tests measured something real and significant.

Theorization: It had become the dominant view – the doxa – that intelligence testing was valid. This was the background intellectual climate for the assessment of Stanley and others.

Perhaps what psychiatrists like Boycott and school medical officers like Thomson brought to any diagnostic encounter was not radically different from assumptions elsewhere in popular culture. What may have been important was the air of scientific legitimacy they lent to these discussions, an expertise that made possible particular kinds of legislation. The punitive segregation policies of the 1920s and the 1930s, for example, required a clear delineation of the distinction between the normal and the defective child, between the educable and the ineducable.[35] It is at least likely that Boycott's medical training and his asylum career meant that he assumed that such a distinction existed, was identifiable and warranted separate systems of care and education for young people. After all, these were the assumptions built into mental deficiency legislation and the growth and development of special schooling from the early 20th century. Such assumptions were contested, of course, not

Theorization on the use of scientific legitimacy and medical status in the construction of ideas about educability.

---

[34]James Kerr (1926) *The Fundamentals of School Health*. George Allen and Unwin, p. 435.

[35]Deborah Thom (1995) 'Mental retardation', in G.E. Berrios, E. German and R. Porter (eds), *A History of Clinical Psychiatry: The Origin and History of Psychiatric Disorders*. London: Athlone, p. 255.

least by Binet and Simon, French pioneers of intelligence testing who were outspoken in their criticisms of the vague and relativistic medical terminology that was capable of wide variations in interpretation.

Despite this imprecision, there was a general allegiance to the idea that mental defect was innate and its aetiology inherited. Perhaps this explains why doctors, who were encouraged to use some version of the intelligence tests that were becoming widely available, often did not do so. Instead, there remained a significant commitment to what were considered the visual signs of deficiency.[36]

Theorization on the ways in which ideas on the heritability of intelligence were used. Confidence of medics to make their own assessments.

All this helps to explain how in 1937, almost 45 years after his graduation and over ten years after his retirement, Norman Boycott came to examine Stanley. No medical records have been located that document that examination and exactly what took place is likely to remain obscure. Yet it has been possible to suggest what Boycott was supposed to be looking for and to explore the influence of the wider medical and social context on his practice. Engaged to inspect the health of school-children and working with a medicalized notion of deficiency that preached the danger of such children in the community, Boycott was asked by a local head teacher to inspect Stanley. This request must itself be understood in the context of a zealous school medical officer who had pushed a reluctant education committee to provide expensive residential provision for mentally deficient children. It is perhaps not surprising that Stanley was diagnosed as mentally deficient and recommended for transfer to special school.

Theorization: This is a key paragraph, tying together the nature of the developing medical doxa about 'subnormality' with the medical officer's examination of Stanley.

Challenging the state

If the recognition of parental rights under the terms of the 1914 Education Act was somewhat ambiguous, it did provide the potential to challenge the growing influence of the state in the private sphere of the family. That potential was, of course, constrained by class and gender. Challenging the law, and the medical expertise on which it depended, required specific knowledge, attitudes and dispositions and it was extraordinarily expensive. Moreover, in patriarchal social systems the rights of the family were usually assigned to men who had control over property,

Theorization: The new rights of parents begin to be discussed as context for an understanding of the Keasley family's resistance to authority.

---

[36]Jackson, M. (2000) *The Borderland of Imbecility: Medicine, Society and the Fabrication of the Feeble Mind in Late Victorian and Edwardian England*. Manchester: Manchester University Press, Chapter 4.

income and material resources and whose authority was sanctioned in law and in a range of social
practices. Indeed, it may be that it is the con-
straints of these rights, and the fact that mothers
dominated exchanges with welfare agencies, that
explains the marginalization of resistance and,
more specifically, fathers as actors in the classification of children.[37]

The prospect of a legal challenge from the parents of Stanley Keasley must have seemed
remote. Stanley's father had regular employment as a printer but the family were not wealthy
and had no significant disposable income. He
had no direct experience of the law and he was
not an autodidact able to draw on independent
learning.[38] It seems that any explanation of the
legal challenge that followed Stanley's diagnosis must consider not just the legally sanctioned
public role of the father, but changing interwar
models of masculinity, domesticity and the ways
in which they were lived by individuals. In other
words, whilst fathers may have been legally
empowered to act in certain ways in the public
sphere, their willingness and capacity to do so
was conditioned not just by material factors but
by changing discourses of masculinities and their
impact on emotional states and experiences.
The latter have escaped sustained scholarly
attention in Britain, not only because of the elusive character of feelings but also because there
is an abiding tendency to see men as only public actors. However Michael Roper has recently
suggested that familial relationships may have
a foundational significance for explaining social
action.[39] Moreover, there is evidence to suggest
that in working-class families fathers were not
the geographically and emotionally distant cari-
catures suggested by Victorian separate spheres
models.[40] Instead, and as Megan Doolittle has
recently suggested, irregular work patterns

Theorization: The changing place of the father in the family, with an attempt to understand Stanley's father's assiduity in challenging the state.

---

[37]Ian Copeland (1999) *The Making of the Backward Pupil in Education in England 1870–1914*. London: Woburn Press has no space for parental agency.

[38]Author's interview with Marie Clarke and Peggy Gageley, Harpenden, 25 January 2008. Transcript and correspondence in author's possession.

[39]Michael Roper (2005) 'Slipping out of view: subjectivity and emotion in gender history', *History Workshop Journal*, 59: 59.

[40]Trev Lynn Broughton and Helen Rogers (eds) (2007) *Gender and Fatherhood in the Nineteenth Century*. Palgrave.

and relative poverty encouraged interdependence and intimacy in working-class families.[41] But quite how this and the heightened interwar discourse on the domestic male impacted on the emotion of fatherhood remains unexplored. Perhaps it was the depth of family relationships, and particularly the relationship between father and son, that help explain the extraordinary response to Stanley's diagnosis.

Shortly after the initial diagnosis, Stanley's father was interviewed by an unnamed official of either Hertfordshire County Council or Harpenden Urban District Council. At the meeting, his father is reported as saying the boy was not feeble-minded and that this view was supported by both his own medical officer and a medical attendant at the Ear, Nose and Throat Hospital, London. Stanley's sisters recall what may well have been this interview as a vigorous argument between their father and the School Board Man who had come to deliver the news that Stanley was an imbecile.[42]

Theorization on the place of the father, with the use of evidence gathered by the author from witnesses who observed Mr Keasley arguing with council officers.

Stanley's father wrote to the Local Education Sub-Committee in October 1937 to confirm his objections to the diagnosis. That letter is reported to have stated that both a General Practitioner and the surgeon who had operated on Stanley judged him 'not deficient in any way', but that 'the father would not incur the expense of forwarding a Doctors report'.[43] At the request of the County Council, the Local Education Sub-Committee summoned Stanley's parents to a meeting designed to persuade them to agree to Stanley's transfer to a local special school. The minutes of the committee report that 'the father attended and stated he was not prepared to agree to the boy going [to the special school]. He also promised to forward certificates to this effect from a specialist and his local doctor'.[44] By December no such certificates had been provided.

Theorization on the place of the father and his determination.

[41]Megan Doolittle (2008) 'Working class fathers, domestic authority and the poor law in England 1870–1910', unpublished paper presented to the European Social Science History Conference, University of Lisbon.

[42]Author's interview with Marie Clarke and Peggy Gageley, Harpenden, 25 January 2008. Transcript and correspondence in author's possession. On the changing image and responsibilities of the School Attendance Officer see Nicola Sheldon (2007) 'The school attendance officer 1900–1939: policeman to welfare worker', *History of Education*, 36(6): 735–46.

[43]HRO, HEd 5/13/3 Local Education Sub-Committtee minutes, 19 October 1937.

[44]HRO, HEd 5/13/3 Local Education Sub-Committee minutes, 16 November 1937.

Stanley appears to have been examined once again by Dr Boycott in May 1938 who once again diagnosed him as feeble-minded. That second examination prompted the threat of legal proceedings to compel attendance at special school 'in the interests of the child'. Yet alongside this threat, however, the education authorities continued to try and persuade. To this end the County Council recommended that 'a lady member of the sub-committee should first see the parents again ... with a view to persuading them, in the interests of the child, to attend [special school]'.[45] In July two women members of the Local Education Sub-Committee:

Theorization: Authority trusting in its agent (the medical officer) rather than hearing the father.

... reported the interview [they] had with the parents from which it appeared the father was still unwilling to allow the boy to attend [special school] and has also made certain complaints as to the treatment of the boy by the Head Teacher. The Committee, after hearing the Head Teacher, decided that the statements of his father were without foundation.[46]

Use of evidence: Documentary evidence taken from the minutes of a council meeting.

In a third and final examination on 5 October 1938, Dr Boycott examined Stanley again. He reported: 'no improvement since he was examined last May and should now be classed as an imbecile. He is not educable at a special school: but should benefit at an occupational centre'.[47] As the Certifying Medical Officer, Dr Boycott signed a certificate of imbecility within the meaning of the 1913 Mental Deficiency Act and this was countersigned by Dr Hyslop Thomson as the School Medical Officer. The County Council are recorded as making arrangements for Stanley's removal from school to the local mental hospital.[48] That removal never occurred. The next reference to Stanley in the education records of the local committee shows that the certificate of deficiency had been quashed and that arrangements were being made for Stanley's return to school.

Use of evidence: Intransigence of the medical officer.

The High Court hearing took place on 25 and 26 April 1939. The intervening period must have been extremely difficult for Stanley's family, and especially his father who was concerned for the

Narrative of next events as court case is heard in London.

---

[45]HRO, HEd 5/13/3 Local Education Sub-Committee minutes, 21 June 1938.

[46]HRO, HEd 5/13/3 Local Education Sub-Committee minutes, 19 July 1938.

[47]HRO, HEd 5/13/3 Local Education Sub-Committee minutes, 18 October 1938.

[48]HRO, HEd 5/13/3 Local Education Sub-Committee minutes, 18 October 1938.

future of his son, subjected to repeated attempts to persuade and cajole acceptance of the diagnosis and unsure about the outcome of the legal challenge he had mounted. In any case Stanley's sisters remember their father departing for London when the case was to be heard, dressed smartly and disappearing for almost a week whilst the fate of their brother was discussed and decided.[49]

In explaining their decision to quash the certificate of deficiency, both Judges Humphreys and Singleton referred to how the 1913 Mental Deficiency Act section 31 provided that where there was doubt as to the educability of any child, the matter would be referred to the Board of Education.[50] Given that there clearly was some doubt based on what appeared to be diametrically opposed medical opinions, both judges expressed surprise and concern that the Board of Education had not been consulted at any time. In fact, it emerged in Court that Stanley's father had expressly made this request but it was ignored.[51]

Narrative: Judges overrule local authority.

The legal ruling was careful to avoid taking a view on the different medical opinions that were expressed. Instead the ruling concerned the production of the certificate. It became clear during questioning that only one of the two medical signatures on the certificate – that of the certifying officer – had actually examined the child. Judge Humphreys called it 'an illustration of an internal administrative system. In plain English, the name of Dr Hyslop Thomson appears on that certificate as certifying this child to be an imbecile when ex concessis he had never even seen the lad'. Judge Singleton – a man of 'stout Lancastrian common sense' according to one biographer – continued:

Narrative: Judge rules that decisions were made improperly.

'It is admitted that this court has power with regard to that certificate, and, there being that power, I think that we should be failing in our duty if we failed to quash that certificate, which, going forth to any one or, to any body of persons, would lead him or them to think that the boy had been examined by two doctors, both of whom certified he was an imbecile. No such state of things existed.

Use of evidence from the judgement.

---

[49]Author's interview with Marie Clarke and Peggy Gageley, Harpenden, 25 January 2008. Transcript and correspondence in author's possession.

[50]Rex v. Boycott and Others. [1939] 2 K.B. 651.

[1]Rex v. Boycott and Others. [1939] 2 K.B. 656–7.

I hope that never again will it be found that a doctor has put his hands to a certificate of that kind without realizing what it means, and how it may be interpreted by others.'[52]

Yet this powerful rebuke heralded no significant changes in policy or practice. Instead, the Board of Education took the opportunity to remind some Local Education Authorities that there was nothing in the recommended arrangements to 'countenance the signing of the Certificate by a second practitioner who has not examined the child'.[53] However, at the same time as rejecting the suggestion that practices of notification exceeded their legal powers, correspondence in the Board of Education files at the National Archives reveals continued uncertainty into wartime at the legality of both diagnostic and regulatory practices.[54] Despite public insistence that there was no need to change policy and practice, and almost 25 years after a senior Board of Education official had confidently predicted narrowing down problematic diagnosis, progress was proving elusive.[55]

Theorization: Resilience of the Local Authority in the face of the judgement against them.

Mental deficiency, psychologies and childhood

The representation of feeble-minded children as a danger to the community, their identification by medical and educational professionals and their removal to specialist institutions are themes now fairly well established in the historiography of western European and North American education. However, our knowledge of these processes remains at a fairly generalized level. Specific accounts of how these processes worked out in practice at the local level remain scarce. This attempt to recount and explain the experience of one child deemed mentally deficient in Britain in the 1930s lend itself to some wider reflections on mental deficiency, psychologies, administration and childhood.

Justification for the case study in the lack of knowledge about how identification and segregation happened in practice.

---

[52]Rex v. Boycott and Others. [1939] 2 K.B. 665–6. For a short biography of Singleton see Hodson (2004) 'Singleton, Sir John Edward (1885–1957)', rev. Alec Samuels, in H.C.G. Matthew and Brian Harrison (eds) *Oxford Dictionary of National Biography*. Oxford: OUP. Available at: www.oxforddnb.com/view/article/36111 (accessed 11 September 2009).

[53]National Archives, Education (ED), 50/268. 'Mentally Defective Children 1939–43'; Board of Education to Herts and Kent Local Education Authorities, 17 May 1939.

[54]NA, ED, 50/268 'Mentally Defective Children 1939-43' (see above).

[55]NA, ED 50/112. Minute by G.E. to Sir George Newman (Chief Medical Officer), 16 September 1920.

The construction of mental deficiency has to be understood against a wider history of state formation. In Koven and Michel's terms a relatively weak central state like Britain continued to rely on local government and private welfare organizations to develop and deliver social policy.[56] This helps to explain both the level of diversity one sees in British welfare provision and the continued importance of volunteer social administrators and professional experts in its application. So whilst Hertfordshire clearly represents a district in which policies of institutionalization and segregation were favoured, there are other places where community care was much more important. However, the relative absence of both detailed local studies and comparative national work means that diversity of provision and practice has not been fully explored nor adequately explained. The political and cultural investments in the project of social science that were routine for major industrializing centres in Europe and North America present some explanatory possibilities, but pursuing these will require comparative work and greater attention to the ways in which different spaces interpreted and developed specific ideas and practices.

Theorization on the construction of mental deficiency, particularly by local authorities – which are many and diverse. Hence the diversity in provision and practice.

People were central to the process of transferring, adapting and applying ideas to social policy. It follows that both individual and collective biographies have the potential to complicate generalized pictures of the twin processes of educationalization and medicalization that were undoubtedly significant in this period.[57] Even a brief reconstruction of Norman Boycott's career, for example, casts some doubt on the idea that physicians working in the educational sphere were somehow more optimistic and more humanistic than medics employed in other areas. Indeed, Boycott's peripatetic employment as a school medical officer suggests that the institutional boundaries between medicine and education, and between psychiatry and psychology, were porous. But because so little is known about the careers of those first generation school medical officers, many of them women, there is no way

Theorization on 'educationalization' and 'medicalization' and the interaction between these in the development of ideas about 'deficiency' and school placement.

---

[56]Seth Koven and Sonya Michel (eds) (1993) *Mothers of a New World: Maternalist Politics and the Origins of Welfare States.* London: Routledge.

[57]Marc Depaepe (1998) 'Educationalisation: a key concept in understanding the basic processes in the history of western education', *History of Education Review*, 27(2): 16–28; Stephen Petrina (2006) 'The medicalisation of education: a historiographic synthesis', *History of Education Quarterly*, 46(4): 503–1.

of estimating how widespread this kind of movement was, nor evaluating how the education and professional experiences of these doctors impacted on the practice of identifying mentally deficient children.

Another observation concerns the significance and use of these artefacts and social technologies. On the whole the explanatory potential of administrative, educational and medical sources has been hampered by a combination of archival and theoretical conservatism amongst historians; this helps account for the dominance of institutional histories in this area. However, the graphs, charts and record cards co-authored by teachers, doctors, and volunteer case workers act as a 'mediator between categories of social actors', they take on some of the properties of historical actors, making problems visible, circulating them for inscription and action.[58] The certificate issued by the medical authorities in this case can be constructively considered in just this fashion: it identified Stanley as a particular type, a child visualized on the page and whose ability to practise normality was severely curtailed. Dr Hyslop Thomson did not need to see Stanley in order to know him. It is tempting to interpret this extraordinary state of affairs biographically; a result of Thomson's particular brand of missionary zeal. Yet an understanding of historical context, a reading of this practice against the growing power of the science of childhood, is far more persuasive and offers evidence of a damaging scientism sweeping Europe and North America in the 1920s and 1930s.

Analysis: Reflection on the use of evidence in this and similar cases – there has been 'conservatism' among historians, who have eschewed the use of 'social technologies'. Here, though, different kinds of evidence provide new kinds of understanding.

In the midst of this scientism, resistance remained possible and is demonstrable. This usually came in fugitive form; moving house, for example, to escape the jurisdiction of a particular local authority. However, the Keasley case was unusually public. The decision to threaten and then enact legal protection against the local authority was both extraordinarily brave and, as far as this author is aware, unprecedented in this field in England. It is also significant that the certificate of mental deficiency issued to Stanley was quashed on what amounts to a technicality. The High Court judges explicitly avoided any comment on Stanley's condition; they saw this as

Concluding theorization on the nexus of authority power which acted to make and legitimate 'mental deficiency' and the unlikely circumstances in which this power nexus was ultimately challenged.

---

[58]Andre Turmel (2008) *A Historical Sociology of Childhood: Development Thinking, Categorization and Graphic Visualization*. Cambridge: Cambridge University Press, p. 120.

the expertise of the medical profession and were no doubt cognizant of the fact that, under the terms of the 1914 Elementary Education (Defective and Epileptic Children) Act, there was no legal machinery to review or appeal the original diagnosis.[59] As a result, it is hard not to find in this case confirmation of the growth of medicine in the field of education. Where a zealous local authority was determined to implement seemingly progressive welfare measures, was willing to ignore the protests of family and eschew the advice of the Board of Education, there was little that could be done to legitimately prevent the institutionalization of a family member. Were it not for the legal challenge, Stanley would have completed his schooling at a residential special school. Instead, his formal schooling remained incomplete but he remained at home, living in the community and eventually went on to long employment with the local authority.

In recent years psychology's influence over education policy, parenting and childhood has taken a distinctively positive form. Instead of identifying difference, positive psychology studies normality, seeking to understand the components of a meaningful and happy life. In classroom applications, positive psychology seeks to develop those skills and attributes that will foster emotional well-being through the life course. This certainly seems like a more progressive and optimistic form of psychological regulation than was apparent in the interwar period. But perhaps Stanley Keasley's story serves as a reminder that faith in science, and scientific method, has frequently outstripped convincing demonstrations of either its accuracy or validity. In this case at least, familial affection, and time and patience, seems to have been a more reliable and benign guide to educational potential.

Concluding theorization on the power of the putatively scientific discourse and the need for respect for the validity of non-expert, family opinion.

Conclusion

In terms of the typology (see Figure 7.2), the *Contesting Certification* case study is, first, an outlier case study, selected because it presents an unusual set of circumstances (Mr Keasley challenged authority in an extraordinary way, given his own circumstances), which enable the inquirer to gain perspectives from the peculiar circumstances of this situation.

---

[59]Ezra Hasson (2005) 'Risk, modernity and history', *International Journal of Law in Context*, 1(4): 315–34.

Second, it serves a purpose (i.e. it is instrumental).

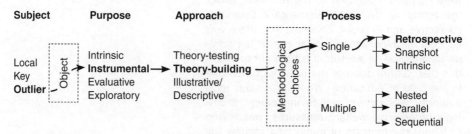

Figure 7.2 Myers's case study *Contesting Certification*

Third, it builds theory, and note that the theory-building occurs throughout the analysis, which happens as the discussion progresses. That discussion is of the subject of the study considered in the context of the theoretical issue which has been identified in the introduction of the article, and which has emerged as a problem, a gap, a dilemma from that background.

Stemming from this issue, the narrative and analysis proceed and it is important to remember that the analysis emerges out of the story being told. In a case study the story is part of the analysis. Bruner goes so far as to say that narrative is at the heart of all meaning-making: 'The process of science-making is narrative ... we play with ideas, try to create anomalies, try to find neat puzzle forms that we can apply to intractable troubles so that they can be turned into soluble problems' (Bruner, 1997: 126).

The choice of methods to be used became clear at several points as the author discussed these, and as primary or secondary sources were drawn upon.

Last, the *process* is simple: it is a single case study reflecting on an historical set of events and biographies. It is retrospective.

The themes which are connected in any case study – selection, narrative, theorization – are evidenced well in this piece of research.

EIGHT

Conclusion: drawing from the anatomy and constructing the study

We have stressed in this book so far various elements in the anatomy of the case study as a form of inquiry: the need for an analytical frame as well as a subject; theorization; generalization; and a range of other issues. It is time now to put all of this together. How might a case study be designed and constructed, knowing what we do about this inquiry form's anatomy?

The construction of the study: Phase 1 – locating a subject and an object

As we have noted throughout the book, an understanding of the separation of subject and object is crucial for the would-be case inquirer in education. A case study, as a *study* (as distinct from a case illustration or a case history) must in some sense explicate a wider theme: it must help in our understanding of some theoretical issue.

So, this is the first thing that needs to be done: to specify the subject and the object. Mrs Smith or Mrs Smith's class of students are not sufficient on their own to constitute case study. They must be cases *of* something. If we now introduce an '*of*' – such as the notion *of* 'class enquirer' (this notion of 'class enquirer' is taken from the ORACLE project's categorization of teacher styles – see Galton et al., 1980), Wieviorka's (1992) call for a 'theoretical, scientific basis' for a study is satisfied. We are now seeing Mrs Smith's class [subject] as a case *of* the class enquirer teacher style [object].

Selection of a subject

Subjects may be persons, groups, time periods, places, events, institutions or any of a range of phenomena that can be studied in their complexity, and, in some sense, their wholeness.

There are, broadly speaking, three grounds for selection of a case subject:

1. A case may be selected because the researcher is intimately connected with it, enabling her or him to 'soak and poke', as Fenno (1986, 1990) puts it; this is a *local knowledge case.*
2. A case may be selected because it is a conspicuously good example of something in which the researcher is interested; this is a *key case.*
3. A case may be selected because it is different from what is typical: it is an 'outlier'; this is an *outlier case.*

The conceptual path that the intending case researcher might follow in coming to a conclusion about these is summarized in Figure 8.1.

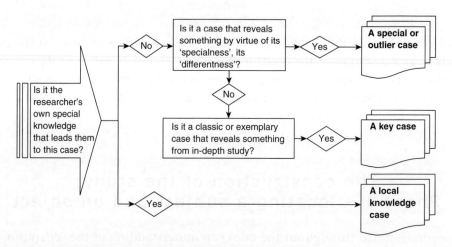

Figure 8.1   Where is the study coming from? The subject

Outlining the object – theory-testing or theory-building

When Wieviorka (1992) drew his distinction between the different ingredients of a study – the practical unity and the 'theoretical, scientific basis' – his emphasis in the second part (the part we have labelled the object) is on the wider body of knowledge, both in practical and theoretical terms, surrounding the subject. How is this 'theoretical, scientific basis' for the study to emerge?

Theory has many meanings in social research (Thomas, 1997, 2007). When we talk of theory in case study we are talking of analysis that seeks connection – that seeks to conjoin ideas and find explanation. Case study cannot be taken to be a form of inquiry without such theorization. Without it, the case study is merely illustration. The analysis, the theorization, is the *object* of the study.

It is a particular kind of theory, though. As we were at pains to point out in Chapters 3 and 4, one interpretation of 'theory' concerns its summative and predictive power, and this stems from expectations of generalization. But generalization is not what we can expect from case study. With this form of research we have to de-couple from expectations about generalization and induction – the building blocks of what Cicourel (1979) called 'strong theory'. The kind of theory we are talking about here, as we made clear in Chapters 3 and 4, is more concerned with the connections and insights it offers between another's experience and one's own. It could perhaps be called 'phronesis' or 'weak theory'.

It is this kind of theorization that is the key to good case study. As Becker (1998: 41) notes, such theorization is a complex process. The connections we seek in offering explanation should be multi-stranded and multi-directional, he suggests. As he puts it:

> ... there are many modes of connection, for which we use words like 'influence' or 'causality' or 'dependence.' All these words point to variation. Something will vary and something else, dependent on what happens to the first thing, will undergo some change as well. (Becker, 1998: 41)

The notion of simple 'causality', he argues, is inappropriate in these circumstances. The distinction between theory-*testing* and theory-*building* case study rests in the firmness of expectations about the intellectual framework that garners these connections and supports and guides the work. Is this framework something which is set at the outset – a set of ideas to be tested by the case study (theory-testing) – or will it be built as the study progresses (theory-building)?

Theory-testing

The assumption here is that there is already some sort of explanatory framework available – the researcher's own, or that provided by others' work – for the phenomenon or situation under study. The case study is being undertaken to test this explanatory framework, this 'theory'.

Theory-building

Theory-building is about developing a scaffold of ideas, a model that somehow 'unwraps' the subject for the explication of the object. So, in a theory-building case study the researcher will be building a framework of ideas that has no necessary connection to pre-formulated notions about what is important. While it may be impossible for the researcher not to connect to pre-existing ideas at all (see Thomas and James, 2006), it is, however, possible to *attempt* to dismiss any allegiance to pre-existing ideas. Researchers attempting to build theory should, in other words, be open to new interpretations suggested by their data.

The construction of the study: Phase 2 – the kind of study

A useful function of the term *subject* is that it serves to make it clear that the focus of interest can be plural: it is not necessarily one person, one event or one phenomenon. There may be more than one: there may, in other words, be different *elements* to the subject of the case study.

Single studies

The single case could be said to be the classic form of the case study. When people think about case studies they think of one person – a patient in a hospital, for example, or a child in a school, or a classic legal case. The single thing is studied for the lineaments of its structure, its character.

Single studies, containing no element of comparison, will take essentially three forms, wherein features of the subject are bounded by time in some shape or form. The case inquirer notices change as it happens and seeks its antecedents and its consequences. We have to find the 'sequence of steps' as Becker puts it (1992: 209) and understand cause in relation to time, with 'each step understood as preceding in time the one that follows it'. In doing this we conjecture not only about how one thing is related to another, but also about how cause and effect change with time as other elements of a situation also change.

The varieties of time-use lead, broadly speaking, to three kinds of study: retrospective, snapshot and diachronic, as we made clear in Chapter 5.

Multiple studies

Multiple studies also take one of the three forms of retrospective, snapshot or diachronic but contain more than one element in their subject. If this is so – that is, if there are two (or several) case subject elements – each individual case element is less important in itself than the comparison that it offers with the others.

If the subject comprises different elements, how can these elements be used for comparison? There are two principal means of doing this:

- Comparison may occur by straightforward contrast between clearly different examples – a simple comparative study. For example, a study might be conducted of two schools' different capacities for making effective use of a visiting education support service. By contrasting the schools' 'biographies' – their histories, catchments, staff relationships and other characteristics – light would be thrown on the relative dynamics affecting the reception and use of the support service. The key focus would not be on the nature and shape of relationships per se in one school, but rather on the nature of the difference between the one and the other and what this might tell us about the dynamics that were significant in this difference.
- Comparison may be of elements within one broader case – comparison, in other words, of nested elements. With nested studies the breakdown is within a larger unit of analysis – for example, classes (the nested elements) within a school (the larger unit). A nested study is distinct from a simple comparative study in that it gains its integrity, its wholeness from the wider case. The elements are nested only in the sense that they form an integral part of a broader picture.

A further subdivision may be drawn in the multiple study, and this is between parallel and sequential studies. In the parallel study, the cases are all happening and being studied at the same time, while with the sequential study the cases happen consecutively and there is an assumption that what has happened in one or in an intervening period will in some way affect the next. Figure 8.2 summarizes the choices made in undertaking single or multiple case studies.

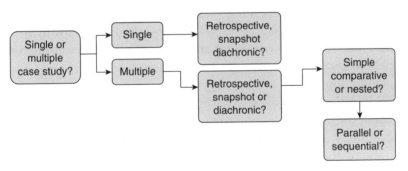

Figure 8.2 Choices in undertaking single or multiple case studies

To close this section, we should note that categorization of form at the outset of a study is not crucial to the study's success. It is not essential correctly to label a case as, for example, a 'key' case or an 'outlier' case. These are categories into which a study is put for the benefit of understanding what is going on and what alternatives are open to the inquirer. More important than correct categorization is to know how a starting point sets off a design track that lets questions be answered in the most fruitful way. The categorization of case studies merely provides a set of options, a menu, through which the researcher may look. It should not be a straitjacket.

The construction of the study:
Phase 3 – intuition, theorization
and analysis

Thinking about how we should foster an intuitive mindset has not been a central consideration in the social sciences. The social sciences have become obsessed with correctness, reliability and design exactitude at the expense of imagination and intuition. This leads ultimately to an inward turn wherein there is more concern for process than there is for questions, arguments, theorization and conclusions. The consequence is that curiosity in inquiry is diminished and research becomes less interesting.

The critic of social science Stanislav Andreski says that how we achieve creativity ...

> ... is just as much a mystery [today] as it was in the days of Socrates: all that is known is that, in order to conceive fruitful original ideas, one must have talent, must immerse oneself in the available knowledge, and think very hard. (1972: 108)

Is Andreski right about this? Can we really not offer useful advice on creativity and intuition? In large part he *is* right. In the final line of his *Tractatus* Wittgenstein said, 'Whereof one cannot speak, thereof one must be silent' (see Kenny, 1993: 31). Wittgenstein was saying a little more than just 'Be quiet if you have nothing to say'. Included in what he was saying is this: some things are beyond our words; they exist in what the philosopher Michael Polanyi (1958) has called 'tacit knowledge'. Included in tacit knowledge are one's knowledge about how to ride a bicycle and one's intuition about how to solve difficult puzzles. What case study offers here is the capacity – or, better, a predilection – to see wholes, rather than fractured parts, and with this predilection we can perhaps have some expectation of a greater emphasis on intuition. Let us think about the practicalities of intuition and theorization a little more.

Good case study is characterized by detailed, sometimes intricate observation of the fabric and texture of a particular situation, 'thick description', and analysis that seeks connection – that seeks to conjoin ideas and find explanation. Case study cannot be taken to be a form of inquiry without such theorization. Without it, the case study is merely illustration. The analysis, the theorization, is the *object* of the study. It is this theorization that is the key to good case study.

In the examples of classic case studies given in Chapters 6 and 7 we have noted how narrative melds into theorization. It is often difficult to separate the one from the other. As an example, Geertz's (1973) classic account of a Balinese cockfight is a stunning narrative in itself, but one in which theorization is effortlessly (and almost poetically) combined with the account. When Geertz tells of one of the Balinese men he is observing taking the bird 'between his thighs, bouncing it gently up and down to strengthen its legs, ruffling its feathers with abstract sensuality' the reader can almost see and smell the scene. He notes that each cock is a 'symbolic expression or magnification' of the owner's self. It is, 'the narcissistic male ego writ out in Aesopian terms'. Geertz's analysis bursts with ideas, theorization – about the culture's relationship with animals, about prestige, about ethics, about aesthetic theory – which are juxtaposed, played with, integrated and fused. It's an essay into which Geertz brings not just his own self, but the ideas of figures as different as Jeremy Bentham, W.H. Auden, Fyodor Dostoyevsky and W.B. Yeats. He concludes by saying that we need analysis which immerses itself in the substance of the subject rather than seeking 'reductive formulas' which profess to account for something.

In Chapter 2 we looked at the ways in which some sociologists such as Erving Goffman organized their view of the world around *dramaturgy*. This is one form of theorization, and one that is worth examining in some more detail for it has been used not just by Goffman but also by a range of interpretivist social scientists. They talk about actors, roles and stages in their discussions of the interactions that take place among people. The case study can be thought of as a play, a drama, complete with:

- a script, a plot and a *leitmotif* (provided by life and the world)
- a stage and scenery (the wider context)
- a *dramatis personae* (a list of characters, institutions or agents)
- a director (the researcher)
- an audience (the readers).

The likening of case study to drama is useful not just because it stresses the bounded nature of study but also because it emphasizes the narrative of the study. In a play, a story is told, a drama, with a beginning, a middle and an end. We noted in Chapter 4 how Bruner drew attention to the lineaments of such narrative and how this can be used in inquiry. There are arguments and links intertwined through any story – a plot, with questions, premises, intrigues, subterfuges. Characters come to life as they deal with the obstacles that the plot puts in front of them. The case study is similar.

The key in theorization is being intuitive and imaginative. As Becker (1998: 7) put it: '[We need] ways of expanding the reach of our thinking, of seeing what else we could be thinking and asking, of increasing the ability of our ideas to deal with the diversity of what goes on in the world.' In Chapter 1 we noted that Einstein had said of the process of science, 'There is no logical path, but only intuition' and this sentiment, in the obsession of social science to be methodologically exact, rigorous and innovative, has sometimes been forgotten. The philosopher of science Karl Popper (1968: 32) made a comment similar to Einstein's: '... there is no such thing as a logical method of having new ideas, or a logical reconstruction of this process. My view may be expressed by saying that every discovery contains "an irrational element", or "a creative intuition".' He proceeds to liken this to Einstein's comment (in an address on Max Planck's 60th birthday) that scientific advance depends on '... intuition, based upon something like an intellectual love (*"Einfuhlung"*) of the objects of experience'.

So, whether in social science, natural science or just inquiry generally it seems to be intuition and *intellectual love* that we have to nurture in seeking understanding and explanation. A tough call, perhaps, since intuition and intellectual love are qualities that don't grow on trees and nor do they lend themselves to bullet-pointed breakdown. Given the elusive nature of intellectual love, imagination and intuition, how should we consider them and how should we foster them in nurturing theory?

For practical advice on this, Sennett (2009: 211) talks about intuition coming in three main stages:

- First from imagination, depending on looking back on sensations already experienced – depending, in other words, on memory.
- Second from establishing adjacency, similar to analogy, where two unlike ideas are brought together.
- Third from surprise, which comes from 'dredging up tacit knowledge into consciousness to do the comparing'.

All of this is similar to the 'imagery' that Becker (1998: 12) speaks about. He suggests that in studying society we start with images and end with them. Our aim '... is the production and refinement of an image of the thing we are studying'.

And theorization is separate from regularization and the drawing of hard and fast, law-like conclusions. The great historian R.G. Collingwood (1994 [1946]), in *The Idea of History*, compared the approaches to history of Herodotus and Thucydides and concluded that Herodotus contributed so much more because '... what chiefly interests Herodotus is the events themselves; what chiefly interests Thucydides is the laws according to which they happen' (ibid: 30). Thucydides's problem, Collingwood suggests, is that he '... is constantly being drawn away from the events to some lesson that lurks behind them' (ibid: 31). Collingwood favours Herodotus's critical narrative-questioning as a way of doing history. He notes: 'In reading Thucydides I ask myself, What is the matter with the man, that he writes like that?'. He answers that Thucydides abandoned history for a kind of pseudo-psychology: 'It is not history at all, but natural science of a special kind. It does not narrate facts for the sake of narrating facts. Its chief purpose is to affirm laws' (ibid: 29).

Collingwood seems to be speaking straight to the case inquirer here. He seems to be saying 'be more like Herodotus'. Herodotus asks us to look with him at the facts; he may tell us what he believes but he will invite readers to make their own judgements. The lawyer Thomas Geoghegan (2007) puts it this way: '... we should also spend more funds to get our young people out of the library where they're reading Thucydides and get them to start living like Herodotus – going out and seeing the world.' This is surely a motto for the case inquirer.

Case study offers the opportunity to bring evidence together from many and varied sources to support arguments in ways that would not be possible using other forms of inquiry that are fenced-in by different considerations. Concerns about how far we can generalize from case study become neutralized when we realize how tentative *any* generalization might be in social research. Conclusions drawn from case study research become less contentious when we realize that to a greater or lesser extent all forms of inquiry, especially social inquiry, produce knowledge that is provisional – in other words, good for only as long as we find out something else that explains things better.

Concluding comment

Case studies have provided some of the most striking insights into social life. Examples are everywhere and some illustrations of exemplary case study are given in Chapter 6. Iconic examples include *Boys in White* (Becker et al., 1976), *A Glasgow Gang Observed* (Patrick, 1973), and Paul Willis's (1993) *Learning to Labour,* which have become classics, each doing much for our understanding of the ways that social life happens. These models of the form have achieved this by painting pictures in fine-grain detail about the encounters that occur between people. All of them enable researchers to keep in contact with the subjects of their studies rather than pretend distance and disinterestedness. Case studies of this calibre allow researchers to think with their own experience and their own intelligence. In some cases they enable a major re-appraisal of the ways in which we build ideas about social life.

While case inquiry may often rely on observation, and to an extent description, these are not ends in themselves and the best case studies go much further than mere illumination. They excavate, elaborate and explicate, offering to researchers a form of inquiry that promises kinds of understanding not accessible through other kinds of research. For this to occur, though, the inquirer needs to understand that there are some key ingredients to good case study research with key distinctions to be drawn among various case study structures and numerous valid permutations of these structures open to the case inquirer. We hope that we have pointed to the ways in which some of these might be constructed.

References

Abbott, A. (1992) 'What do cases do? Some notes on activity in sociological analysis', in C.C. Ragin and H.S. Becker (eds), *What is a Case? Exploring the Foundations of Social Inquiry*. Cambridge: Cambridge University Press, pp. 53–83.

Acemoglu, D. and Robinson, J.A. (2012) *Why Nations Fail*. London: Profile Books.

Acemoglu, D., Johnson, S. and Robinson, J.A. (2003) 'An African Success Story: Botswana', in D. Rodrik (ed.), *In Search of Prosperity: Analytic Narratives on Economic Growth*. Princeton, NJ: Princeton University Press, pp. 80–122.

Althusser, L. (1979) *For Marx*. London: Verso.

Alvesson, M. and Sköldberg, K. (2000) *Reflexive Methodology – New Vistas for Qualitative Research*. London: SAGE.

Andreski, S. (1972) *Social Sciences as Sorcery*. London: André Deutsch.

Back, S. (2002) 'The Aristotelian challenge to teacher education', *History of Intellectual Culture*, 2(1). Available at: www.ucalgary.ca/hic/files/hic/back_forum.pdf (accessed 27 September 2009).

Bacon, F. (1999 [1605]) *Advancement of Learning*. Whitefish, MT: Kessinger Publishing.

Bacon, F. (1854 [1620]) 'Novum Organum', in B. Montague (ed. and trans.), *The Works*. Philadelphia: Parry & MacMillan. Available at: http://history.hanover.edu/texts/Bacon/novorg.html (accessed 31 December 2013).

Ball, S. (1981) *Beachside Comprehensive: A Case-Study of Secondary Schooling*. Cambridge: Cambridge University Press.

Barker, R.G. (1968) *Ecological Psychology*. Stanford: Stanford University Press.

Barrow, J. (1997) *The Values of Science*. Oxford: The Amnesty Lectures.

Barthes, R. (1974) *S/Z* (trans. R. Miller). New York: Hill and Wang.

Bassey, M. (1999) *Case Study Research in Educational Settings*. Maidenhead: Open University Press.

Bassey, M. (2001) 'A solution to the problem of generalization in educational research: fuzzy prediction', *Oxford Review of Education*, 27(1): 5–22.

Bates, R.H. (1998) 'The International Coffee Organization: An International Institution', in R.H. Bates, A. Greif, M. Levi, J.L. Rosenthal and B. Weingast (eds), *Analytic Narratives*. Princeton, NJ: Princeton University Press, pp. 194–230.

Bates, R.H., Greif, A., Levi, M., Rosenthal, J.L. and Weingast, B. (1998) *Analytic Narratives*. Princeton, NJ: Princeton University Press.

Bateson, G. (1999 [1972]) *Steps to an Ecology of Mind*. Chicago: University of Chicago Press.

Becker, H.S. (1992) 'Cases, Causes, Conjunctures, Stories, Imagery', in C.C. Ragin and H.S. Becker (eds), *What is a Case? Exploring the Foundations of Social Inquiry*. Cambridge: Cambridge University Press, pp. 205–16.

Becker, H.S. (1998) *Tricks of the Trade*. Chicago: University of Chicago Press.

Becker, H.S., Geer, B., Hughes, E.C. and Strauss, A. (1976) *Boys in White*. New Jersey: Transaction Publishers.

Bennett, A., Barth, A. and Rutherford, K.R. (2003) 'Do we preach what we practice? A survey of methods in political science journals and curricula', *Political Science & Politics*, 36(3): 373–7.

Berger, P.L. and Luckmann, T. (1979) *The Social Construction of Reality: A Treatise in the Sociology of Knowledge*. Harmondsworth: Penguin.

Blumer, H. (1992) *Symbolic Interactionism: Perspective and Method*. Berkeley: University of California Press.

Bourdieu, P. (1992) 'The Practice of Reflexive Sociology', in P. Bourdieu and L.D. Wacquant, *An Invitation to Reflexive Sociology*. Chicago: University of Chicago Press, pp. 216–60.

Bronfenbrenner, U. (1979) *The Ecology of Human Development*. Cambridge: Harvard University Press.

Bronfenbrenner, U. and Morris, P.A. (1998) 'The Ecology of Developmental Processes', in R.M. Lerner (ed.), *Handbook of Child Psychology: Vol. 1: Theoretical Models of Human Development*. New York: Wiley, pp. 993–1028.

Bruner, J. (1991) 'The narrative construction of reality', *Critical Inquiry*, 18(1): 1–21.

Bruner, J. (1997) *The Culture of Education*. Cambridge, MA: Harvard University Press.

Bryant, G. and Monk, P. (2001) *Summary of the final report of the investigation into the North Leicestershire cluster of variant Creutzfeldt-Jakob Disease*. Leicestershire: Leicestershire Health Authority. Available at: www.cbsnews.com/htdocs/pdf/vcjd. pdf (accessed 5 January 2010).

Burgess, R.G. (1984) *The Research Process in Educational Settings: Ten Case Studies*. Lewes: Falmer.

Byrne, R.M.J. (2005) *The Rational Imagination: How People Create Alternatives to Reality*. Cambridge, MA: MIT Press.

Caldwell, J.C. (1986) 'Routes to low mortality in poor countries', *Population and Development Review*, 12(2): 171–220.

Campbell, D.T. (1957) 'Factors relevant to the validity of experiments in social settings', *Psychological Bulletin*, 54: 297–312.

Campbell, D.T. (1988) *Methodology and Epistemology for Social Sciences: Selected Papers*. Chicago: Chicago University Press.

Campbell, D.T. and Stanley, J.C. (1966) *Experimental and Quasi-Experimental Designs for Research*. Chicago: Rand McNally.

Carr, W. and Kemmis, S. (1986) *Becoming Critical. Education, Knowledge and Action Research*. Lewes: Falmer.

Checkland, P. (1981) *Systems Thinking, Systems Practice*. Chichester: John Wiley.

Cicourel, A.V. (1979) 'Field Research: The Need for Stronger Theory and More Control Over the Data Base', in W.E. Snizek, E.R. Fuhrman and M.K. Miller (eds), *Contemporary Issues in Theory and Research: A Metasociological Perspective*. London: Aldwych Press, pp. 161–76.

Coles, G. (1987) *The Learning Mystique*. New York: Pantheon Books.

Collingwood, R.G. (1994 [1946]) *The Idea of History*. Oxford: Oxford University Press.

de Vaus, D.A. (2001) *Research Design in Social Research*. Thousand Oaks, CA: SAGE.

Dewey, J. (1920 [2004]) *How We Think*. Whitefish, MT: Kessinger Publishing.

Diamond, J. (2005) *Collapse: How Societies Choose to Fail or Survive*. London: Penguin Books.

Dickens, W.T. and Flynn, J.R. (2001) 'Heritability estimates versus large environmental effects: the IQ paradox resolved', *Psychological Review*, 108: 346–69.

Eckstein, H. (1975) 'Case Study and Theory in Political Science', in F. Greenstein and N. Polsby (eds), *The Handbook of Political Science: Strategies of Inquiry, Vol. 7*. London: Addison-Wesley, pp. 79–137.

Einstein, A. (1936) 'Physics and reality', *Journal of the Franklin Institute*, 221(3): 349–82.

Eisenhart, M. (2009) 'Generalization from Qualitative Inquiry', in K. Ercikan and W.M. Roth (eds), *Generalizing from Educational Research*. London: Routledge, pp. 51–66.

Fenno, R. (1986) 'Observation, context, and sequence in the study of politics', *American Political Science Review*, 80(1): 3–15.

Fenno, R. (1990) *Watching Politicians: Essays on Participant Observation*. Berkeley: Institute of Governmental Studies, University of California.

Ferguson, N. (1999) *Virtual History: Alternatives and Counterfactuals*. New York: Basic Books.

Feyerabend, P. (1993) *Against Method* (3rd edition). London: Verso/New Left Books.

Fish, S. (1989) *Doing What Comes Naturally*. Oxford: Clarendon Press.

Flynn, J.R. (1987) 'Massive IQ gains in 14 nations: what IQ tests really measure', *Psychological Bulletin*, 101: 171–91.

Flynn, J.R. (1998) 'IQ Gains Over Time: Toward Finding the Causes', in U. Neisser (ed.), *The Rising Curve: Long-Term Gains in IQ and Related Measures*. Washington, DC: American Psychological Association, pp. 25–66.

Flynn, J.R. (1999) 'Searching for justice: the discovery of IQ gains over time', *American Psychologist*, 54(1): 5–20.

Flynn, J.R. (2003) 'Movies about intelligence: the limitations of g', *Current Directions in Psychological Science*, 12(3): 95–9.

Flyvbjerg, B. (2001) *Making Social Science Matter*. Cambridge: Cambridge University Press.

Flyvbjerg, B. (2006) 'Five misunderstandings about case-study research', *Qualitative Inquiry*, 12(2): 219–45.

Fodor, J. (2001) *The Mind Doesn't Work that Way*. Cambridge, MA: MIT Press.

Foucault, M. (1981) 'Questions of method: an interview with Michel Foucault', *Ideology and Consciousness*, 8(Spring): 3–14.

Foucault, M. (1991) *Discipline and Punish* (trans. A. Sheridan). London: Penguin.

Gadamer, H.G. (1975) *Truth and Method*. New York, NY: Seabury Press.

Galton, M., Simon, B. and Croll, P. (1980) *Inside the Primary Classroom*. London: Routledge and Kegan Paul.

Garvin, D.A. (2003) 'Making the case: professional education for the world of practice', *Harvard Magazine*, 106(1): 56–107.

Geertz, C. (1973) 'Deep Play: Notes on the Balinese Cockfight', in *The Interpretation of Cultures: Selected Essays*. New York: Basic Books, pp. 412–53.

Geoghegan, T. (2007) 'History lessons: for Americans, Herodotus has better ones to offer than Thucydides', *The American Prospect*. 12 March. Available at: www.prospect.org/cs/articles?articleId=12547 (accessed 27 February 2010).

George, A.L. and Bennett, A. (2005) *Case Studies and Theory Development in the Social Sciences*. Cambridge, MA: MIT Press.

Gerring, J. (2004) 'What is a case study and what is it good for?', *American Political Science Review*, 98(2): 341–54.

Glaser, B.G. and Strauss, A.L. (1967) *The Discovery of Grounded Theory: Strategies for Qualitative Research*. New York: Aldine.

Gomm, R., Hammersley, M. and Foster, P. (2000) 'Case Study and Generalization', in R. Gomm, M. Hammersley and P. Foster (eds), *Case Study Method*. London: SAGE.

Grundy, S. (1987) *Curriculum: Product or Praxis?* London: Routledge.

Haack, S. (2003) *Defending Science – Within Reason: Between Scientism and Cynicism*. Amherst, NY: Prometheus Books.

Haig, B.D. (1995) 'Grounded Theory as scientific method', *Philosophy of Education, 1995: Current Issues*. Urbana: University of Illinois Press, pp. 281–90.

Hammersley, M. (2001) 'On Michael Bassey's concept of the fuzzy generalization', *Oxford Review of Education*, 27(2): 219–25.

Hammersley, M. (2005) 'Assessing quality in qualitative research', Paper presented to ESRC TLRP seminar series: *Quality in Educational Research*, University of Birmingham, 7 July. Available at: www.education.bham.ac.uk/research/seminars1/esrc_4/index.shtml (accessed 20 Sept 2009).

Hammersley, M. (2007) 'The issue of quality in qualitative research', *International Journal of Research and Method in Education*, 30(3): 287–306.

Hammersley, M. and Gomm, R. (2000) 'Introduction', in R. Gomm, M. Hammersley and P. Foster (eds), *Case Study Method*. London: SAGE, pp. 1–16.

Harman, G. (1965) 'The inference to the best explanation', *Philosophical Review*, 74: 88–95.

HEFCE (2009) *RAE 2008 Subject Overview Reports*. Available at: www.rae.ac.uk/pubs/2009/ov/ (accessed 11 June 2009).

Hempel, C.G. and Oppenheim, P. (1948) 'Studies in the logic of explanation', *Philosophy of Science*, 15(2): 135–75.

Hirsch, E.D. (1976) *The Aims of Interpretation*. Chicago: University of Chicago Press.

Holton, G. (1995) 'The controversy over the end of science', *Scientific American*, 273(4): 168.

Houser, N., Kloesel, C. and the Peirce Edition Project (eds) (1992) *The Essential Peirce* (2 vols). Bloomington, IN: Indiana University Press.

Jenkins, R. (1992) *Pierre Bourdieu*. London: Routledge.

Johnson, S. (1963 [1759]) 'The Idler, no. 58, Universal Chronicle', in W.J. Bate, J.M. Bullitt and L.F. Powell (eds), *Works of Samuel Johnson Vol. 2*. London: Yale University Press.

Johnston, P.H. (1985) 'Understanding reading disability: a case study approach', *Harvard Educational Review*, 55(2): 153–77.

Kahneman, D. and Tversky, A. (1973) 'On the psychology of prediction', *Psychological Review*, 80(4): 237–51.

Kenny, A. (ed.) (1993) *The Wittgenstein Reader*. Oxford: Blackwell.

Köhler, W. (1925) *The Mentality of Apes*. New York: Harcourt.

Kuhn, T.S. (1970) *The Structure of Scientific Revolutions*. Chicago: University of Chicago Press.

Kundera, M. (1984) *The Unbearable Lightness of Being* (trans. Henry Heim). London: Faber and Faber.

Latour, B. and Woolgar, S. (1979) *Laboratory Life: The Social Construction of Scientific Fact*. Beverly Hills, CA: SAGE.

Leakey, L.B. and van Lawick, H. (1963) 'Adventures in the search for man', *National Geographic*, 123(1): 132–52.

Lewin, K. (2008 [1946]) *Resolving social conflicts / Field theory in social science*. Washington, DC: American Psychological Association.

Lijphart, A. (1971) 'Comparative politics and the comparative method', *The American Political Science Review*, 65(2): 682–93.

Lincoln, Y.S. and Guba, E.G. (1985) *Naturalistic Inquiry*. Thousand Oaks, CA: SAGE.

Lipton, P. (1991) *Inference to the Best Explanation*. London: Routledge.

Luker, K. (2008) *Salsa Dancing into the Social Sciences: Research in an Age of Info-Glut*. Cambridge, MA: Harvard University Press.

Lynch, M. (1985) *Art and Artifact in Laboratory Science*. London: Routledge.

MacIntyre, A. (1985) *After Virtue: A Study in Moral Theory*. London: Duckworth.

Makkreel, R.A. and Rodi, F. (eds) (1991) *Wilhelm Dilthey: Selected Works, Volume I: Introduction to the Human Sciences*. Princeton, NJ: Princeton University Press.

Mandel, D.R., Hilton, D.J. and Catellani, P. (2005) *The Psychology of Counterfactual Thinking*. London: Routledge.

Medawar, P.B. (1982) *Pluto's Republic*. Oxford: Oxford University Press.

Merriam, S.B. (1988) *Case Study Research in Education: A Qualitative Approach*. San Francisco, CA: Jossey-Bass.

Miller, S. and Fredericks, M. (1999) 'How does grounded theory explain?', *Qualitative Inquiry*, 9: 538–51.

Mitchell, J.C. (2006) 'Case and situation analysis', in T.M.S. Evens and D. Handelman, *The Manchester School: Practice and Ethnographic Praxis in Anthropology*. Oxford: Berghahn Books, pp. 23–43.

Mogey, J.M. (1955) 'The contribution of Frédéric Le Play to family research', *Marriage and Family Living*, 17(4): 310–15.

Mouzelis, N. (1995) *Sociological Theory: What Went Wrong?* London: Routledge.

Murdoch, I. (2002) *Under the Net*. London: Vintage.

Myers, K. (2011) 'Contesting certification: mental deficiency, families and the state', *Paedagogica Historica: International Journal of History of Education*, 47(6): 749–66.

Nadel, S.F. (1957) *The Theory of Social Structure*. London: Cohen and West.

Oakeshott, M. (1967) *Rationalism in Politics and Other Essays*. London: Methuen.

Oakley, A. (1999) 'Paradigm wars: some thoughts on a personal and public trajectory', *International Journal of Social Research Methodology*, 2(3): 247–54.

Parlett, M. and Hamilton, D. (1972) 'Evaluation as Illumination': *New approaches to the study of innovative problems* (Occasional Paper No. 9). Edinburgh: Centre for Research in the Educational Sciences, University of Edinburgh.

Pascal, B. (2005 [1658]) *Pensées* (trans. Roger Ariew). Indianapolis: Hackett Publishing Company.

Patrick, J. (1973) *A Glasgow Gang Observed*. London: Methuen.

Peirce, C.S. (1992 [1878]) 'How to Make our Ideas Clear', in N. Houser and C. Kloesel (eds), *The Essential Peirce, Vol.1*. Bloomington, IN: Indiana University Press, pp. 124–41.

Plato (2004) *Protagoras and Meno* (trans. R.C. Bartlett). New York, NY: Cornell University Press.

Polanyi, M. (1958) *Personal Knowledge: Towards a Post-Critical Philosophy*. London: Routledge and Kegan Paul.

Pólya, G. (2004 [1945]) *How to Solve it*. Princeton: Princeton Science Library.

Popper, K.R. (1968). *The Logic of Scientific Discovery*. London: Hutchison.

Popper, K.R. (1977) 'On hypotheses', in P.N. Johnson-Laird and P.C. Wason (eds), *Thinking: Readings in Cognitive Science*. Cambridge: Cambridge University Press, pp. 264–273.

Ragin, C.C. (1992) 'Introduction: Cases of "What is a Case?"', in C.C. Ragin and H.S. Becker (eds), *What is a Case? Exploring the Foundations of Social Inquiry*. Cambridge: Cambridge University Press, pp. 1–18.

Ragin, C.C. (2007) 'Comparative Methods', in W. Outhwaite and S.P. Turner (eds), *The SAGE Handbook of Social Science Methodology*. Los Angeles: SAGE, pp. 67–81.

Ragin, C.C. and Becker, H.S. (eds) (1992) *What is a Case? Exploring the Foundations of Social Inquiry*. Cambridge: Cambridge University Press.

Rodrik, D. (ed.) (2003) *In Search of Prosperity: Analytic Narratives on Economic Growth*. Princeton, NJ: Princeton University Press.

Rorty, R. (1982) *Consequences of Pragmatism (Essays: 1972–1980)*. Minneapolis: University of Minnesota Press.

Ryle, G. (1990) *The Concept of Mind*. London: Penguin.

Sacks, O. (1996) *An Anthropologist on Mars*. London: Picador.

Schatzman, L. (1991) 'Dimensional analysis: notes on an alternative approach to the grounding of theory in qualitative research', in D.R. Maines (ed.), *Social Organisation and Social Process: Essays in Honor of Anselm Strauss.* New York: Aldine, pp. 303–14.

Schön, D.A. (1987) 'Educating the reflective practitioner', Presentation to the Annual Meeting of the American Educational Research Association, Washington, DC.

Schutz, A. (1964) 'The Stranger: An Essay in Social Psychology', in *Collected Papers, Vol. II. Studies in Social Theory.* The Hague: Martinus Nijhoff, pp. 91–105.

Schwandt, T.A. (2001) *Dictionary of Qualitative Inquiry* (2nd edition). Thousand Oaks, CA: SAGE.

Sen, A. (1999) *Development as Freedom.* New York: Alfred A. Knopf.

Sennett, R. (2009) *The Craftsman.* London: Penguin.

Simon, H. (1983) *Reason in Human Affairs.* Oxford: Basil Blackwell.

Simons, H. (1996) 'The paradox of case study', *Cambridge Journal of Education,* 26(2): 225–40.

Simons, H. (2009) *Case Study Research in Practice.* London: SAGE.

Smail, D. (1993) *The Origins of Unhappiness.* London: Harper Collins.

Smith, L.M. (1978) 'An evolving logic of participant observation, educational ethnography, and other case studies', *Review of Research in Education,* 6(1): 316–77.

Stake, R. (1978) 'The case study method in social inquiry', *Educational Researcher,* 7(2): 5–8.

Stake, R.E. (1995) *The Art of Case Study Research.* Thousand Oaks, CA: SAGE.

Stake, R.E. (2005) 'Qualitative Case Studies', in N.K. Denzin and Y.S. Lincoln (eds), *The SAGE Handbook of Qualitative Research* (3rd edition). Thousand Oaks, CA: SAGE, pp. 443–66.

Stenhouse, L. (1978) 'Case study and case records: towards a contemporary history of education', *British Educational Research Journal,* 4(2): 21–39.

Stenhouse, L. (1980) 'The study of samples and the study of cases', *British Educational Research Journal,* 6(1): 1–6.

Storr, A. (1997) *Feet of Clay: Study of Gurus.* London: Harper Collins.

Tavor Bannet, E. (1997) 'Analogy as translation: Wittgenstein, Derrida, and the law of language', *New Literary History,* 28(4): 655–72.

Thomas, G. (1997) 'What's the use of theory?', *Harvard Educational Review,* 67(1): 75–105.

Thomas, G. (2002) 'Theory's spell – on qualitative inquiry and educational research', *British Educational Research Journal,* 28(3): 419–34.

Thomas, G. (2007) *Education and Theory: Strangers in Paradigms.* Maidenhead: Open University Press.

Thomas, G. (2010) 'Doing case study: abduction not induction; phronesis not theory', *Qualitative Inquiry,* 16(7): 575–82.

Thomas, G. (2011a) 'The case: generalization, theory and phronesis in case study', *Oxford Review of Education,* 37(1): 21–35.

Thomas, G. (2011b) 'A typology for the case study in social science following a review of definition, discourse and structure', *Qualitative Inquiry,* 17(6): 511–21.

Thomas, G. (2012a) 'Changing our landscape of inquiry for a new science of education', *Harvard Educational Review*, 82(1): 26–51.

Thomas, G. (2012b) *How to Do your Case Study – A Guide for Students and Researchers.* London: SAGE.

Thomas, G. (ed.) (2013a) *Case Study Methods in Education: Volume Three: The Case Study in Practice – General Issues and Specific Examples.* London: SAGE.

Thomas, G. (ed.) (2013b) *Case Study Methods in Education: Volume Four: Examples of Case Studies in Education.* London: SAGE.

Thomas, G. and James, D. (2006) 'Re-inventing grounded theory: some questions about theory, ground and discovery', *British Educational Research Journal*, 32(6): 767–95.

Thomas, G. and Loxley, A. (2007) *Deconstructing Special Education and Constructing Inclusion* (2nd edition). Maidenhead: Open University Press.

Thomas, G., Walker, D. and Webb, J. (1998) *The Making of the Inclusive School.* London: Routledge.

Thomas, W.I. and Znaniecki, F. (1958 [1927]) *The Polish Peasant in Europe and America* (2nd edition). New York: Dover.

Turney, J. (2004, April 23) 'Private eye with "helps to inquiry"' [Review of the book *Defending Science – Within Reason: Between Scientism and Cynicism,* by S. Haack (2003)]. *Times Higher Educational Supplement.* Available at: www.timeshigher-education.co.uk/story.asp?storyCode=188226&sectioncode=39 (accessed 31 December 2013).

VanWynsberghe, R. and Khan, S. (2007) 'Redefining case study', *International Journal of Qualitative Methods*, 6(2): 80–94.

Vaughan, D. (1992) 'Theory Elaboration: The Heuristics of Case Analysis', in C.C. Ragin and H.S. Becker (eds), *What is a Case? Exploring the Foundations of Social Inquiry.* Cambridge: Cambridge University Press, pp. 173–204.

Vickers, G. (1965) *The Art of Judgment: A Study of Policy Making.* London, Chapman and Hall.

von Bertalanffy, L. (1950) 'The theory of open systems in physics and biology', *Science*, 111: 23–9.

Vygotsky, L.S. (1978) *Mind in Society: Development of Higher Psychological Processes.* Boston, MA: Harvard University Press.

Wacquant, L.D. (1989) 'Towards a reflexive sociology: a workshop with Pierre Bourdieu', *Sociological Theory*, 7: 26–63.

Waismann, F. (1984) *Ludwig Wittgenstein and the Vienna Circle: Conversations Recorded by Friedrich Waismann.* Oxford: Basil Blackwell.

Wallace, W.L. (1969) *Sociological Theory.* London: Heinemann.

Walton, J. (1992) 'Making the Theoretical Case', in C.C. Ragin and H.S. Becker (eds), *What is a Case? Exploring the Foundations of Social Inquiry.* Cambridge: Cambridge University Press, pp. 121–37.

Welton, D. (ed.) (1999) *The Essential Husserl.* Bloomington, IN: Indiana University Press.

White, H.C. (1992) 'Cases are for Identity, for Explanation, or for Control', in C.C. Ragin and H.S. Becker (eds), *What is a Case? Exploring the Foundations of Social Inquiry*. Cambridge: Cambridge University Press, pp. 443–66.

Wieviorka, M. (1992) 'Case studies: history or sociology?', in C.C. Ragin and H.S. Becker (eds) *What is a Case? Exploring the Foundations of Social Inquiry*. Cambridge: Cambridge University Press, pp. 159–72.

Willis, P. (1993) *Learning to Labour*. Aldershot: Ashgate, pp. 62–77. [First published by Saxon House, 1978.]

Wittgenstein, L. (1958) *The Blue and Brown Books*. Oxford: Blackwell.

Wormald, B.H.G (1993) *Francis Bacon: History, Politics and Science, 1561–1626*. Cambridge: Cambridge University Press.

Wrong, D.H. (2003) *Reflections on a Politically Skeptical Era*. Edison, NJ: Transaction Publishers.

Yin, R.K. (2003) *Case Study Research: Design and Methods*. Thousand Oaks, CA: SAGE.

Yin, R.K. (2009) *Case Study Research: Design and Methods* (4th edition). Thousand Oaks, CA: SAGE.

Zigler, E. and Muenchow, S. (1992) *Head Start: The Inside Story of America's Most Successful Educational Experiment*. New York: Basic Books.

Index